How to Analyze People

The Little-Known Secrets to Speed Reading a Human, Analyzing Personality Types and Applying Behavioral Psychology

Contents

Introduction

What if I told you that you've just made one of the best decisions of your life by reading this book? Well, that's what is happening! If there is one thing successful, powerful people understand about the game of life, it's that life is about people. Scratch that — it's about understanding how the human mind works.

Fortunately, like any skill, you can learn how to analyze people and read people quickly.

Why should you want to learn? Well, it's not all about just influencing people — although if you did pick up this book to learn that, then it is on you to use what you learn for the right reasons, *and not to foster hate.* When you know how to analyze people, you are in a relevant position in society, in that you'll always know how to foster harmony wherever you go.

You know how to get grown adults (who are hollering at each other) to shut up, sit down, and find the similarities in their seemingly different views. You also know how to get your three-year-old to eat their broccoli, even if they're not totally in love with the unpopular veggie.

In this book, we will talk about how you can scientifically analyze people as you interact with them. You will learn to read their body language and the meaning back of the words they say. You'll get a handle on their mannerisms. You're not going to get a certificate for human behavioral psychology by reading this, but by the end of this book, you will understand what it's all about. You will learn and see in others (or yourself) how psychology comes to play in our daily lives in ways that are obvious - and not quite as obvious.

No two individuals are exactly alike — except perhaps those spooky twins from that popular horror movie. So, it matters that you learn about the basic types of human personality, and how you can connect with each. You'll learn what unique gifts these personalities bring to the table. Even more, you will learn how to weave your different personality with another's so you can both work and live together in harmony, experiencing mutual benefit from each other.

How is this book different? There are lots of books out there on the same topic, but this one is up-to-date, without fancy words you have to keep Googling, and there are useful, practical methods you can apply right away to your daily life.

Whether you're reading this book because you want a better love life or you want to be a better friend or colleague, again, you've made the right choice. Once you're finished, you will find that you're much better at observing things you'd have missed before. You'll be able to read people with as much ease as you're reading the words on this very page!

No matter the situation you're faced with, whether bad or good, you'll know how to handle it a lot better, maintaining an objective viewpoint. This results in better relationships, and ultimately, a higher quality of life. Isn't that something we could all use?

Now, let's begin.

Chapter One: The Benefits of Analyzing Others

What does it mean to analyze someone? It's not about squinting your eyes just so and trying to see through to their dark, twisted soul. The human behavioral analysis involves trying to make sense of the chaos that is the way the human mind works. It's about understanding not just what we think about, but why we have the habits of thought and behavior that we do. It's about understanding the way that these thoughts affect our daily choices, both the deliberate ones and the not-so-deliberate ones.

It's about the science (and art) of psychoanalysis, which you can thank Sigmund Freud for. "Psychoanalysis" is derived from the Greek words psykhé which means "soul," and análysis, which means "investigate." You might say it involves a sort of soul-peering.

There are several schools of thought with psychoanalysis, from Freud to Jung. This book isn't about getting into all that detail. You want to learn to read people, and that's what we shall focus on.

How Psychologists Analyze You

So, your buddy Siobhan is a clinical psychologist. You've always wondered if you need to have your guard up around her. Finally – and courageously – at a party with friends, you ask her, "Hey Siobhan! Are you always analyzing me?"

Well, if she was honest, she'd tell you that yes, she is analyzing you. However, she isn't. Let's get into this ultra-confusing answer I've given you. The job of a clinical psychologist is to pay attention to behaviors, mannerisms of speech, and irregular actions.

Let's say that Siobhan sees someone acting weirdly, saying some really out-there things, then she will definitely take interest and analyze the heck out of them. It's not because she's trying to be a creep, but because she's been trained to analyze behavior. So, even if she wasn't actively analyzing you at that moment, she's analyzing you now, because you've brought her attention to you. She might be wondering how many martinis you've pounded back, whether you're under the influence of something else, or you're simply experiencing an episode of mania.

Now, here's why she says she *isn't trying* to read you. She could do a cold read if she wanted to, but from a professional standpoint, the only way to get a grasp on what you're thinking and feeling is to ask you questions. Go figure.

Often, people seek the help of a clinical psychologist when they're facing some challenge in their relationships, at work, or when things are just not going the way they feel they should. Naturally, the professional psychologist won't just do a cold read. They will ask you questions before they diagnose whatever it is you're troubled by (depression, anxiety, bipolar disorder, and so on).

Even then, the diagnosis is only the start. It gives Siobhan a context for the challenges you're facing and gives her a clue of the treatments you'll need. However, it does little for letting her know the reason you're experiencing these issues or how she can give you a designer treatment for your case.

The psychologist must go even deeper. They'll have some analyzing to do, often covering these aspects:

Origins: They could discuss what growing up was like for you so they can see where the start of your issues lies. They'll want to know about any genetic disorders, what your childhood and family were like, anything of significance that happened to you as a kid, and things of that nature.

Accelerants: These are the changes you might have recently experienced that has caused these problems to surface or made them even worse than usual.

Mechanisms: These cause your issues to happen. The mechanism is literally that: A machine, built from your origins, fueled by your accelerants so that when turned on, they instantly cause these problems of yours to go from zero to ninety in half a millisecond.

Let's look at this in action. Say you have issues with loneliness, underdeveloped social skills, physical, and social anxiety. Those are the problems.

The origins of the problems could be that your family has a history of anxiety, and you never got out much. You only ever spent time with your family, so you didn't learn the basics of getting to know others or communicating with others.

Now let's look at the mechanisms of your possibly fictional anxiety issues. Anxiety is a condition that mostly affects the social sphere of life, surfacing only when you're involved in social situations. Because of this, you make a point of staying away from Thanksgiving dinner, because you just can't handle it. Because of your inability to say hello (like a regular person) to the people around you, you develop a view about yourself that you're "weird."

What accelerates these problems you have? You probably had something trigger depression in you when you were in high school, and since then, you've constantly been worried about your issues getting even worse — and they do, inevitably. I should clarify that this example is oversimplified. Humans are complex. It's not easy to find precisely one reason for why we do the things we do.

One-Tenth of a Second

When you meet someone, you unconsciously and immediately form an impression about them based on your preconceptions of life and the patterns people should conform to. Anecdotally, it takes a little under a minute to size someone up. But the brilliant psychologists at Princeton have studied this phenomenon thoroughly and have found it takes a whopping one-tenth of a second to form your first opinion about someone while relying mostly on body language.

So ,what happens after that first impression has been made? Well, every other impression is still mostly based on nonverbal communication. Dr. Albert Mehrabian, in his wonderful book *Silent Messages*, suggests that all that chit-chat and banter between you and the other person only makes up a grand total of 7 percent of all communication you share. The rest of it is from nonverbal cues (body language and facial expressions), and vocal cues.

Because of all this, the question then becomes, how good are you at reading other people, really? If you miss out on the remaining 93 percent of the communication equation, then chances are you're not that great at figuring others out. No worries. You're going to learn how to do that in this book.

Why You Should Learn to Read People

It doesn't matter what profession you're in, or your status in life. The ability to read others around you is a skill with unparalleled benefits. It's like a superpower!

Say you're a radio presenter, and you've been given a script to work with as you interview some businessperson or celebrity. You could be very efficient about your job, sticking to the script, never deviating. That's great! But, what if you could read people?

You'd be able to tell when your guest has a lot more to say on a certain subject, go off script, and get some new angle no one's ever gotten from them. You'd be able to tell when a certain line of questioning is causing them to clam up, so you can back off, or rephrase the question in a less antagonistic way. This is just a small way that behavioral analysis can help you.

When you understand the remaining 93 percent of communication, there's a world of difference in every aspect of life. It could be the difference between moving forward in your career or remaining stuck in the muck. It's how you get ahead of the curve in your field. It's the reason your boss trusts you with more responsibility and promotes you – or doesn't.

Reading people correctly can save you a ton of heartbreak. Imagine a world where everyone figured out on the first date whether a relationship with the person sitting across from them was worth pursuing. See? No heartbreaks. All dates would end with a handshake, and "Let's do this again, never."

The ability to analyze people correctly and clearly means you can easily settle issues at home. You can keep the peace with your employees or colleagues at work. Don't go through unnecessary, rowdy, sometimes violent arguments, unless you're into that or some reason (in which case, you need to read a different book and see a mental health professional).

Reading people is a skill that anyone and everyone will reap benefits from. Salespeople and advertising companies know the value of grasping behavioral psychology. Don't be surprised that these companies will happily hire people with a degree in psychology because they expect them to figure out how to turn basic human behavior into profit.

The human mind and its workings are often being exploited for good or bad. You've been to a store. Have you ever asked yourself why you always make last-minute buys at the checkout counter? It's because things have been deliberately set up that way. Those items were put right in your line of vision, so as you're paying for the stuff you did plan to buy, you wind up thinking, "Meh, might as well get that pack of gum. The babe likes that."

Are You a Master People Reader?

Some people think that they are absolute pros at reading others. You've probably been in this situation: You're at a party, sipping on your drink, taking it all in, feeling at one with yourself and the universe at that moment. How blessed you are to know such awesome people! Suddenly, some random person walks up to you and asks, "Hey, what's with the long face?"

You tell them that you're fine, but they insist you can't be because you're looking so down. You offer the classic line, "This is my happy face," but they do not believe it. They've probably even pulled up a chair to sit by you so you can talk about your deep, dark problems. Well, if you weren't sad before, you're sad now. Maybe, you can relate to this experience. Maybe, you've even been guilty of this mistake yourself.

So, here's a quiz for you to figure out just how great you are at reading people on a basic level, with no crystal balls. Many of these feelings are often misinterpreted. You have four options for each question. Try to see how many you can accurately answer. Watch someone you know well. Analyze them. Then ask them how they are feeling. Did you get it right?

1. Fear. Embarrassment. Surprise. Anger.
2. Politeness. Interest. Happiness. Flirtatiousness.
3. Disgust. Sadness. Anger. Pain.
4. Amusement. Sadness. Shame. Embarrassment.
5. Contempt. Pride. Anger. Excitement.
6. Interest. Fear. Compassion. Surprise.
7. Contempt. Sadness. Disgust. Shame.
8. Anger. Disgust. Pain. Sadness.
9. Flirtatiousness. Embarrassment. Love. Desire.
10. Pain. Anger. Sadness. Shame.
11. Anger. Compassion. Interest. Sadness.
12. Desire. Excitement. Amusement. Surprise.
13. Interest. Happiness. Desire. Surprise.
14. Shame. Compassion. Sadness. Disgust.

15. Love. Desire. Disgust. Contempt.
16. Sadness. Shame. Embarrassment. Pride.
17. Compassion. Happiness. Desire. Politeness.
18. Love. Embarrassment. Shame. Sadness.
19. Sadness. Guilt. Disgust. Pain.
20. Satisfaction. Compassion. Love. Flirtatiousness.

Chapter Two: Understanding Human Behavior & Psychology

We all hold strong opinions about such things as whether the death penalty should remain, whether the church and state should mingle and whether there should be pineapple on pizza. These are attitudes we all have around certain issues. These attitudes can dictate what you believe and how you behave, as well. Let's talk about attitude some more.

The Psychologist's Definition of Attitude

Psychologists say attitude is the tendency to judge things, issues, people, and events in a light, whether good, bad, or uncertain. Attitude comprises three components:

> • The affective component, being how you feel about the person, thing, or issue in question.
> • The behavioral component, which is how your attitude affects your behavior.
> • The cognitive component, which involves your beliefs and thoughts on the matter.

These are the ABC's of attitude.

Attitude can also be looked at in terms of being explicit and implicit. Where implicit attitudes are just beneath the surface, unconscious, they still affect our patterns of belief and the way we behave. Explicit attitudes are those we know of, which obviously affect our thoughts and actions.

Your attitude can be because of experience, sociocultural norms, and learned behavior from, say, the classical conditioning that advertisers use on us to get us to think about things a certain way. You can also develop an attitude, thanks to operant conditioning, which involves getting feedback from your environment about your behavior. Your attitude could also result from simple observation of everyone around you, just like how, as a child, you observed your parents and likely took on their beliefs and behaviors in certain situations.

Most folks assume that attitude and behavior are often in line with each other, but that is not the case. For instance, an undercover DEA agent could have an attitude of disgust with drug dealers and illegal substances, but that doesn't mean they're going to immediately cuff everyone they know is a dealer. In the same way, you may strongly support a candidate, but you might not necessarily go out to vote.

Behavior Analysis

Behavior analysis is based on the tenets of behaviorism. There are three ways psychologists analyze behavior:

- Experimentally investigating behaviors.
- Applying learned facts about behavior to real-world contexts.
- Analyzing behavior based purely on concepts, theoretically, historically, philosophically, and methodologically.

Techniques for Behavior Analysis

To make things even more practical, here are the techniques used by the pros to analyze behavior:

1. **Prompting**: The behavior analyst will trigger the response they seek by using a prompt. This prompt could be a visual cue or a verbal cue.

2. **Chaining**: Here, the behavior analyst turns a task into chunks, smaller bits. The easiest of the tasks (or the first one) will be taught first. As soon as that task has been handled, then they can move on to the next, creating a chain that only ends when the sequence is complete.

3. **Shaping**: The behavior in focus is altered bit by bit. With each step the subject takes toward the preferred behavior, there is a reward.

Your Brain and Your Behavior

Biopsychology studies how your brain, it's neurotransmitters (or chemicals) and other parts of your body affect your thoughts, feelings, and behavior. This field is also called behavioral neuroscience.

The point of this study is to analyze the way the biological processes in your brain work with cognitions, emotions, and all other strictly mental processes in your brain.

There have been phenomenal discoveries about the way the brain functions based on biological factors. Your spinal cord and brain make up your central nervous system (CNS). Your cerebral cortex, the outer part of your brain, is what handles sensation, cognition, emotions, and motor skills.

Your brain has precisely four lobes:

- The frontal lobe handles high-level cognition, motor skills, and the expression of self through language.

- The occipital lobe helps you understand all information and stimuli visual in nature.

- The parietal lobe is the reason you can process all tactile stimuli, among other things. It's why you know when to get your hand off the hot stove or why that massage feels so good.

- The temporal lobe processes auditory information, helping you understand language and sound. It also helps you with processing your memories, among other things.

You also have a **peripheral nervous system** made up of:

- The sensory or afferent division, which takes all sensory info to your central nervous system for processing.

- The motor or efferent division works to connect your central nervous system to your glands and muscles.

Then there's your **autonomic nervous system** made up of:

- The sympathetic nervous system handles your fight, flight, or freeze reflex in response to danger and stress.

- The parasympathetic nervous system, which brings your body to a restful state and handles your digestive process, among other things.

Within this wonderful brain of yours are chemicals known as neurotransmitters. These take information from neuron to neuron, and for sending information from a brain to a body part, and vice versa. Examples of neurotransmitters are dopamine, which handles learning and movement. When you have too much of that, you're at risk for disorders like schizophrenia. Too little, and you might have to contend with Parkinson's disease.

Dopamine is a feel-good hormone. When you feel good, it's only natural to indulge in behavior that continues to perpetuate that good feeling. In this way, and in so many other ways, your brain affects your behavior. If the frontal lobe was unusual in any way, that would affect the way you think, which would affect your behavior.

Other Factors that Affect Human Behavior

People behave the way they do depend on several other factors besides the brain. Here are some:

- Abilities: These are the things you've learned from observing your environment and the things that you're naturally gifted at. There are three classes of abilities: Intellectual abilities are the sort that involves logic, intelligence, the ability to communicate and analyze. Physical abilities would be your strength, speed, stamina, motor skills, and body coordination. Self-awareness abilities involve the way you feel about the tasks you must do.

- Gender: Whether you're a man or a woman, you've got equal chances as the other to do well mentally, or at a specific job. However, society respects the difference between both. For instance, when a woman is usually the caregiver for kids, it's not unusual behavior for her to be absent from work sometimes.

- Race and Culture: it's not proper to ascribe behavior based on culture and race, but it happens, and this can influence behavior. You may be of a certain race, which has had to deal with certain stereotypes. You're deliberate about behaving differently.

- Perception: Perception is how you turn data from your senses into useful information you can work with. There are six types of perception: The perception of sound, touch, taste, speech, other senses, and the social world.

- Genetics: Your genetic makeup can also influence your behavior. This is because your genes have done an excellent job of preserving the responses your ancestors had to certain situations. For instance, a child's genetic makeup might dictate whether they walk at three months, or eight months. This genetic influence on behavior has larger implications, but thankfully, you don't have to worry. Your behavior can change for the better and is not necessarily set in genes, or stone.

- Environment: The environment plays a huge role in behavior. Take a pair of twins at birth and separate them, one in India and the other in Sweden. They probably would be as different as sky and ground. The cultures in these two places are different, and so behavior would naturally be different to some extent.

The Three Laws of Human Behavior

Law #1: Behavior will often align with the status quo, unless there's a reward or a risk that necessitates change. If you've done something repeatedly, so it becomes a habit that becomes the status quo for you. Think of it like inertia, according to Newton's first law of motion. If your behavior changes, then something must force it to, whether it's a bad thing (like an inability to breathe well if you're a smoker) or a good thing (like a bump in pay raise when you actually give your work your all).

Law #2: Your behavior boils down to your kind of person and your environment. You didn't just drop down to the earth with an already formed set of behaviors. You can thank Kurt Lewin for boiling down behavior to your state or traits, and your environment. These elements are interdependent in that you can't predict behavior based only on your understanding of who someone is, how they think, and feel, nor can you predict behavior based on the environment they're in. You need a combo of both.

Law #3: Every decision you make will have trade-offs and can lead to unplanned consequences. That's just the fact of life. You want to start working out. The pro: you get fit and healthy. The con: you've got to make time for it, maybe go shopping for new gym clothes too. It's all about opportunity cost, or, "What am I sacrificing if I choose to do this thing." There are also consequences you don't intend to have or don't anticipate. For instance, you could decide to workout with some loud music to feel pumped and motivated, but your neighbors might be trying to get some sleep after a long night shift and might not appreciate the noise. That's known as the tragedy of commons.

Techniques Used by Behavioral Psychologists

Here are techniques that behavioral psychologists use which you can implement in your life now:

1. Detangling Cognitive Distortions: You can detangle the errors in thinking you have by yourself, but you must first know the ones you suffer from the most. Here's a quick run-through of possible distortions you might be dealing with:

a) Black-and-white or polarized thinking: You think everything is this or that, and there are no shades of gray, no in-betweens.

b) Filtering: You focus only on the negative aspects of things, instead of the positives and negatives, or vice versa.

c) Jumping to conclusions: You are certain of things with no evidence.

d) Overgeneralization: You take one thing that happened one time with one sort of person and assume that is the law with every other person who looks or sounds like that. Or you assume you failed at a new business, so you'll fail at others.

e) Personalization: You think everything you say or do affects others, even when that's actually an exaggeration. For instance, you assume being late to a party would throw it off schedule.

f) Minimizing or Magnifying/Catastrophizing: You assume that the worst will happen if it hasn't already, all because of an event that's not as terrible as you thought. Or, you assume positive things are not that important, like when you do a stellar job, or you're a great friend.

g) Fairness fallacy: You take the need for everything and everyone to be fair to the extreme, and this makes you unhappy.

h) Control fallacy: You feel like all things that happen either are entirely on you or entirely because of forces beyond your control. You don't allow yourself to think that it could be both not one or the other.

i) *Shoulds*: These are the assumptions and rules you have about how you and others *should* act. When these rules are not followed, you get mad.

j) Blaming: When things don't line up as you expected, you allocate responsibility to someone else or something else besides yourself. Maybe you blame others for the way you act or feel.

k) Change Fallacy: You think people should change to suit your mood. You assume your happiness lies in the way others behave, so if they don't change as you'd like them to, you get upset.

l) Emotional logic: You feel a certain way, so you assume the way you feel must be true. However, emotions are not the best go-to when you want objective truth.

m) The fallacy of "Heaven's Reward": You think that when you deny yourself good things and sacrifice yourself, you'll get a great reward for your selfless deeds. However, when those rewards don't come, you feel bitter.

n) Always being in the right: You find it hard to accept that you could be wrong. It matters deeply that you're always right. Your rightness matters so much that other people's feelings could burn to ashes for all you care. You have trouble accepting you're wrong.

o) Mislabeling or global labeling: This is a generalization to the extreme. You take one or two events or traits, and you project that and make it a universal thing. You failed at riding a bike, so you believe you will fail at swimming and life.

There's also assuming just because someone says something you think is critical or rude, that they're anything but friendly. Often you use overly exaggerated ways to describe that one act they did. Your roommate didn't do the dishes last night? By Jove, what a filthy rat!

2. Cognitive restructuring: This involves looking at how you got these distortions, and why you buy into them. When you discover the beliefs that power them, you can challenge and change them.

3. Journaling: As you journal, you assess your thoughts and moods, and your reactions. There's no better way to get to know yourself, your patterns of thoughts, your emotional leanings, and how to cope with, adapt to, or change them.

4. Nightmare exposure and re-scripting: Dealing with nightmares? Then you can use this technique. You bring your nightmare to mind and let it drum up the emotions you felt. Once you feel the discomfort and fear, you can figure out what you'd rather feel and then create a new image that works with your preferred emotion to replace the nightmare.

5. Interoceptive exposure: This is great for dealing with anxiety and panic. You expose yourself to the bodily sensations you're afraid of, so you can get the usual response. As you do, the toxic beliefs with the sensations arise, and you hold on to the sensation without seeking to avoid them, or distract yourself, so you can learn new things about it. It shows you that your panic symptoms are not life-threatening. Uncomfortable, but not dangerous.

6. Progressive muscle relaxation: Lie in a comfortable position, and then scan your body by muscle group, starting from your toes, to your head. Breathing deeply, you tense each muscle group, and then relax it several times before moving upwards. You can check out YouTube videos for guided relaxation sessions.

7. Exposure and response prevention: If you suffer from obsessive-compulsive disorder, this can help. Expose yourself to the things that trigger your compulsion and do your best to refrain from your usual response. Do this repeatedly. Journal your feelings as you do, and notice as your compulsions weaken.

8. Relaxed breathing: This is a great mindfulness technique. There are so many ways to use this, from guided meditations to un-guided ones. Simply bring your attention to your breath. Breathe in deeply through your nose, and then exhale through your lips, slightly parted. Your exhale will be longer than the inhale. That's okay. This helps with OCD, depression, panic disorder, anxiety, and a host of other illnesses.

9. Relive the scene until the end: This works if you're battling anxiety and fear. It's basically an experiment where you imagine the worst possible scenario of how things could go. It helps you realize that even in the worst case, you will still manage simply fine.

Chapter Three: The 16 Personality Types

Now, let's talk about personality. What is it, really? Personality refers to the differences that exist from one person to another, in terms of their set patterns of thought, emotion, and behavior. Studying personality involves considering the differences that exist in certain personality traits, like being generally irritable or sociable. It's also about understanding how all the various aspects of a person come together to form a complete being.

The Myers-Briggs Personality Types

There are 16 personality types according to the Myers-Briggs classification of personalities. Let's sink our teeth into each one, a la Dracula.

The Architect

This personality is an imaginative and strategic thinker with a plan for just about everything. They are classified as Introverted, Intuitive, Thinking, Judging (INTJ). They are particular about details and have a great way of blending the rational with creativity. You'll find an Architect is a private person, with a rich, complex world within. This personality type is rare and capable of taking on more responsibility than most. The female Architect is almost a unicorn, difficult to find. It's tough for the Architect to find those that can deal with their constant analysis of everything. However, the Architect is not bogged down by analysis. They make swift decisions and are curious, yet focused, and ambitious. You won't find them wasting energy on trivial pursuits like gossip. The Architect is an interesting combination of a dreamer always looking on the bright side and a bitter pessimist. They're very innovative, thanks to their profound insights and logical thinking. They're a perfectionist in all they do. If you can't keep up with them, they will leave you far behind. Do you have rules? Your rules can go hug a powerline. They are not big on social skills. They won't shoot the breeze with you. They love to be out of the spotlight, but this doesn't mean they lack confidence.

The Logician

The Logician is Introverted, INtuitive, Thinking, and Prospecting (INTP). They think on their feet. If you need an unconventional way of looking at things or doing things, you can't go wrong with them. They're almost as rare as the Architect — and that's actually a great thing. The last thing the Logician wants is to be "common." They love that they're the inventive, creative ones, with no-box thinking and an impressive intellect. The logician sees the pattern in everything. They are also quick to see where something doesn't add up, so please don't lie to them. The funny thing about the Logician and lies is that you must be wary of what they say. No, they're not liars, but they open their minds up to you while still working on ideas that still need a lot of working out. Think of yourself as a sounding board to them. Don't take it personally. The Logician may not deliver when they said they would, but they do deliver. They might seem lost in their dreams, but really, they're always thinking. From the second they realize they're awake, ideas flood their minds in torrents. This makes them seem a tad detached, but it's nothing to worry about. They're pretty chill to be around, especially when they're with people who have the same interests, or close and trusted friends. However, the Logician doesn't do well with new people, as they're suddenly shy. Banter can turn to battle if they suspect you're critical of their ideas.

The Inspector

The Inspector is Introverted, Sensing, Thinking, Judging (ISTJ). They can seem a tad intimidating when you're in the room with them, especially when you have no connection or relationship to them. They seem rather proper, serious, and all about formalities. They value all things traditional and old-school. They love the time-honored values of hard work, patience, honor, and responsibility in their society and culture. They are calm, upright, reserved, and thoughtful. Unfortunately, they are often misunderstood.

The Counselor

The counselor is Introverted, Intuitive, Feeling, Judging (INFJ). They have the most brilliant minds and are highly creative. The way they think about things is unusual, and unfortunately, their viewpoint is often misunderstood. The INFJ is about depth with thought and speech. There's got to be substance to whatever currently holds their attention. They're not the kind to be content with the superficial or buy into the shiny bright tinsel you're coating your words with. They are always scanning for much better ways to deal with challenging issues. Some people might think this odd, but that's just the INFJ's ways.

The Giver

Meet the ENFJ: Extroverted, Intuitive, Feeling, Judging. They're the giving type. They're very charismatic and have grand ideas. They're the outspoken person in the room who is bound by ethics and principles. This means that the ENFJ finds it easy to relate with people from all walks of life and all other personality types. They depend on their feelings and intuition much more than the real world. This fondness for their imagination can be problematic for them, and those who deal with them. They're not about living in the now, as they'd rather lose themselves in abstract thoughts about what is possible in the future.

The Craftsman

This is the Intuitive, Sensing, Thinking, Perceiving (ISTP) personality. They have an air of mystery to them that is never unraveled, leaving them misunderstood. While they are all about logical and rational thought, they can quite demonstrate enthusiasm and spontaneity. It's not easy to gauge their personality traits, compared to the other types of personalities. You can't beat yourself up for this, though. Even those who are close to the ISTP can't say with certainty what they will do next. The Craftsman is spontaneous, but they're also crafty at hiding that spontaneity from you and I, preferring to show up as responsible and logical.

The Provider

This Extroverted, Sensing, Feeling, and Judging (ESFJ) personality can't help but be social. They have an innate desire to connect with others socially. They love nothing more than to make others happy, and they're the darlings of the lot. The ESFJ is usually the star of the show, and they always show up for family and friends, whether that means personal needs or setting up social events for everyone to get together. The Provider is loved by most, and it's easy to see why.

The Idealist

Introverted, Intuitive, Feeling, and Perceiving (INFP). These introverts, like other introverts, are reserved and quiet. No, this differs from being shy. The Idealist would rather not make themselves the subject of discussion, especially not when you're just meeting for the first time. You'll find them on their own, in quiet places, which lets them figure out the world they live in. The INFP is a huge fan of symbols and signs, always digging into them to find the actual meaning of their life. It's not hard for the INFP to get lost in their heads. They are The Idealist. This can be a good thing when they put their thoughts to practical use or a bad thing when they wind up drowning in a sea of ideas, fantasies, and other thoughts.

The Performer

Extroverted, Sensing, Feeling, Perceiving (ESFP) - the Performer is just that: An entertainer. They're great at distracting and amusing the rest of us, and they just love to be in the limelight. They're often the one in the middle of a circle of laughing people, recounting tales in the most interesting ways. They are rather thoughtful and incredibly open to exploring the world. They're passionate about learning, and about sharing what they've learned with others. The Performer loves to have company. They're great at social and interpersonal skills. The life of the party, it's never a dull moment with them — and far be it from them to turn down a chance to have all eyes on them. Don't let this put you off, though. The Performer is a warm person. You'll find them quite friendly and generous. Also, if you want a sympathetic ear, then they'll give you both of theirs. This personality cares about how everyone is doing.

The Champion

Extroverted, Intuitive, Feeling, and Perceiving, the ENFP is an individual to the core. They don't follow. They don't fall in line, and they don't give a rip about the status quo. They're the ones who love to rock the boat. They'll find their own way of doing things. They'll find a creative way to wear a boring tie. Their ideas, habits, and actions are anything but regular. The Champion is not fond of people who only color within the lines. Try to make them follow set rules, and they'd be miserable. However, the Champion does enjoy being with the right people, and nothing is more pleasurable than connecting on an intuitive level with others. The ENFP is usually "all in their feels" in the way they do things. It's not a bad thing, actually, since they are thoughtful in their words and actions, and are able to perceive subtext and cues.

The Doer

The Doer is Extroverted, Sensing, Thinking, and Perceiving. They're the reason for the term "social butterfly." They enjoy interacting with people and are energized by emotions and feelings. Now, don't be quick to assume this means the Doer is flippant about life. Far from it. They love reasoning, using logic to arrive at conclusions that make sense — as long as it doesn't keep them from letting their thoughts roam wild and doing what they set out to do. To hold the ESTP's attention, you'd better have more than just abstract ideas and theories for them. They want to go, and they want to go now! They want to act. They're the sort likely to make a move and deal with the consequences as they come up. For them, this is much better than just sitting on their hands or thinking of contingency plans.

The Supervisor

The ESTJ – Extroverted, Sensing, Thinking, Judging - is about traditional values. They love dedication. They treasure truth, honor, and being organized. The Supervisor has an extraordinarily strong moral compass. They will act only if it's right to do so, and whatever they do must be socially acceptable. It's not easy to clearly state the right and the wrong way to do things, but the Supervisor will surely step in to lead the way for everyone else, letting their personal thoughts be known. The Supervisor is the model citizen; the one everyone goes to when they need sound advice. This personality is more than happy to give you the counsel you need.

The Commander

The Commander is an ENTJ – Extroverted, intuitive, Thinking, Judging. They're about dealing with all things around them using discipline and logic. When they've satisfied their need for logic and discipline, then they can allow their intuition to step in. The Commander is a born leader. Of all the personality types, the Commander has leadership in their blood. They're okay with taking charge. Scratch that, they relish the chance to be in charge. The Commander believes in possibilities, so they aren't floored by challenges that come their way. The Commander welcomes problems, seeing them as an opportunity to do and be better. They are unafraid of making the hard decisions, to which they always give a lot of thought. The Commander does not wait for life to happen. They go out there and create opportunities where there seems to be none.

The Nurturer

Intuitive, Sensing, Feeling, Judging, the Nurturer will always be generous. They're the philanthropist, you know, always willing and happy to give back. If you were ever kind to them, then they will return that kindness to you seventy times seven. That's just the way they are. If you're fortunate enough to have the Nurturer believe in you, then trust they will go out for you with no hidden agenda. The Nurturer also upholds the ideals they believe in with that same unbridled passion. They're the kindest, warmest personalities you will ever have the pleasure of knowing. Sensitive to the way others feel, the Nurturer will always hold peace, cooperation, and harmony in high esteem. They're always considerate of others, and very aware of how people around them feel. Also, they can't help but bring out the best in everyone they meet.

The Visionary

This Extroverted, Intuitive, Thinking, Perceiving (ENTP) personality is also rare. They are extroverts, but they don't do well with small talk. Not even a little bit. Because of this, they don't do well at parties or social scenes, particularly when everyone around them is of a quite different personality type than they are. The Visionary is deeply knowledgeable about things. Their intelligence is unparalleled. These two traits make it, so they need constant mental stimulation, so they don't get bored. They love a chance to talk facts and theories, diving into every little detail, making sure you get it right. The Visionary is rational, logical, and objective in how they deal with everything. They approach arguments the same way, so if you ever find yourself in a verbal fencing match with them, know that they expect you to be logical and rational.

The Composer

Say hello to the Intuitive, Sensing, Feeling, Perceiving personality. The funny thing about these introverts is that they don't always seem introverted. Sure, they have some stumbling and fumbling going on when they try to connect with you for the first time, but give them enough time to warm up, and they become very friendly, warm, and approachable. The ISFP is a fun person to hang out with. They can act on a whim, the spontaneous Composer. You'd have a great tie going to various events with them, whether planned or unplanned.

The Composer has one intention: Make the most of life. They are all about being present, and this helps others see the wonder of the ordinary moments they take for granted. The Composer seeks new discoveries and adventures. They value understanding others, as they'll often get great golden nuggets of wisdom from each encounter. So, while they may be introverted, they actually love meeting new people more than the other introvert personalities do.

Tips for Identifying Each Type

1. ISFJs, ESFJs, ISTJs, and ESTJs talk about past stories and experiences. They are practical and often down to earth. They love to hark back to tradition and draw on their personal experiences. They remember what has worked well, and they use that info when it's needed. They love routine and find security in it. These types are loyal, responsible, and dedicated. They love supporting their communities and families.

2. The ESTPs, ISTPs, ESFPs, and ISFPs are great at taking in all the details going on in the now. They are very well aware of their environment and know how to make the present count. They are adventurous, up for a good time, easy-going, and flexible. You will notice that they know how to disentangle themselves gracefully through the obstacles that present themselves physically. They have great spatial awareness and love to engage with the world outside of them, using a hands-on approach. They love to interact with ideas and will take opportunities to act on them.

3. The INFJs, ENFJs, INTJs, and ENTJs are mostly future-oriented. They see the big picture and figure out the possible ways that things will work out by paying attention to clues, patterns, and connections that most people miss. They are drawn to the unknown, the mystical, the existential, and theoretical. They are very single-minded people, with extreme focus and clear-cut plans for the way they want life to go. They often will get an instinctual nudge about how things will work out, or about what steps to take next. Often, these

hunches turn out for the good, even though they seem to come out of nowhere. These types are very intense, so don't let that scare you off.

4. The ISTPs, ESTPs, INTPs, and ENTPs are all about logic. You can tell who they are because they love to learn for the fun of it, not to impress people. They don't want your admiration; they don't care about following rules. These personalities will use language that indicates they create their own destiny as they want to.

5. The ENTJs, INTJs, ESTJs, and ISTJs, are very productive. It's hard to miss their confidence. They plan ahead, and they're all about making things happen in the most efficient way. They want to put their stuff out there. You'll notice they're the ones who don't procrastinate but prefer to get things over and done with way ahead of time.

6. The INFPs, ENFPs, ISFPs, and ESFPs are a unique, authentic lot who care about the values they hold. "To thy own self be true" is their motto if you observe them closely. They're about making an impact for the causes that matter to them. Their morals have nothing to do with where they are, or what society says. They are averse to any fake vibes. Also, they're open-minded, very empathetic, and the best listeners you could ever hope to have. They aren't so quick to share their feelings with people they haven't gotten to know yet.

7. The ISFJs, ESFJs, ENFJs, and INFJs are friendly and full of empathy. They can easily tell what your mood or emotions are. They do their best to maintain upbeat morale wherever they go, with everyone they deal with. No matter who they're talking to, they know how to weave their words in such a way it lands right and has a great impact. For them, it's about values, harmony, and ethics.

Chapter Four: The Secrets of Speed Reading

Speed reading is about figuring out someone's temperament or personality type. You can quickly figure out the sort of person you're dealing with by asking them certain questions. The Myers-Briggs classification of personalities gives you 16 personalities, but they're all in four major classes, so don't be overwhelmed with trying to remember them all. Learn to speed read because it will help you relate better with people.

Breaking Down the Categories of Myers' Briggs

Extrovert/Introvert. This is about what energizes you the most. Do you draw your energy from being with other people? Then you are most definitely an extrovert. If you don't get your energy from being with people, but from being alone, then you're an introvert. Most people erroneously assume that introversion and extroversion are about being outgoing or not. That's not it at all. There are extremely outgoing introverts who are very expressive, believe it or not. Introversion and extroversion come down to your *source of energy*.

Sensory/Intuition. What this category covers is how you absorb information. Do you absorb it internally, allowing your ideas and thoughts to percolate and bubble up from within? Or are you the sort who pays more attention to your five senses? If you're a "thought percolator," then you're intuitive. However, if you primarily get your information from the environment you're in, wherever that is, then you're sensory or "sensing."

Thinking/Feeling. What this comes down to is how you process the information you get. Are you the person who chews on facts, figures, and concrete data before anything else? If this comes naturally to you, then you're definitely "Thinking." However, if you usually first process stuff like emotion, the impact a certain action or event would have on others, values, and things of that nature, then you are "Feeling. "

Judging/Perceiving. This is about how you decide in your day to day life. If you're Judging, you decide faster and earlier. You're very structured, and you love order. You make well-informed decisions way before they're due, and you would much rather decide way before the deadline, and not at the last minute. This way, you can hold on to your structure and the sense of order in your life. The Sensory Judging, in particular, is crazy about lists, as they help them stay organized. If you perceive, on the other hand, then you're a lot more flexible than the Judging. You're so flexible that you tend to wait until the very last minute to decide on something. You do this because you're still acquiring and processing information and resources and getting to know the options available to you.

The reason for this is simple. You want to make sure that you make the most of the time that you've got between the present and the looming deadline to choose the best course of action. You're always about looking for a better solution or fix than what is currently available.

As for the Judging, you are a heavy procrastinator. However, that's not accurate. What's really going on is you need to find the best options because that really matters to you. And, often, you do wind up finding said better options anyway.

Waiting till the last minute does not leave you stressed. The Judging personality would be stressed, having to wait as you do. You, on the other hand, would be stressed out trying to decide early or plan and make lists and get organized. Others would say you perform well under pressure. You probably have the most brilliant ideas when the deadline looms closer.

The thing about these four categories of personalities is that they are not black-and-white. They are preferences or your automatic behavioral response to events in life. It's not like you're strictly an introvert or an extrovert, or strictly a judger or a perceiver.

Think of them as your initial preference, or what you're most naturally inclined to act like. For instance, some extroverts can be fine with being on their own. Some of them voluntarily want to be alone. Go figure. You have two hands. You have the option of using either, but only one hand will be dominant unless you're ambidextrous.

Another thing to note about these categories is that they have scores or grades to them, from zero to thirty. To keep things simple, think of it more like a range from a slight preference to a strong preference. People have their preferences, but they can think through all these categories, and as they mature, they think through the weaker aspects or slight preferences, giving them strength.

Speed Reading People

Extrovert or Introvert?

Say you asked someone this question: When you're tired after a long day and need to unwind, do you prefer to head out to a party at the club, or would you rather go home and be alone?

Assume they answered, saying, "Yeah, I'd rather just go to a coffee shop and be alone." That's a curious answer that's very telling. Say you were to probe further, asking why a coffee shop. They might say, "Well, I like the sounds of other people in the background, but that's it. I actually just want to be by myself while I can hear others." Is this person an introvert or an extrovert? They're extroverted.

Here's another question you could ask when speed reading someone: How often do you like to spend time by yourself? They might say, maybe 20 percent of the time.

Then you can follow that up with this question: When you're alone, how long do you like to spend by yourself until you decide you need company? Even among just extroverts, you would get a variety of answers. Some want to be alone a whole day. Some want to be alone for just 30 minutes. See? Nothing is black and white here. These questions will let you know whether they're extroverts or introverts.

Sensory or Intuitive?

To figure out where someone lies in this category, ask this: When you're learning about your world, do you spend more of your time paying attention to the stuff you can see, touch, and smell, or do you just have ideas that start to well up in your mind and you no longer follow what's happening around you? What describes you best?

Another good question to ask: Do you find it frustrating and downright confusing when you have to deal with way too much theory?

Here's another question: Are you better at coming up with original ideas, or would you rather implement them?

If you're dealing with a sensory person, then you've got to communicate with them in concrete terms. If you're dealing with intuitive, they love to have fun with ideas, but they're great at taking an abstract idea and making it concrete — unless they're on the extreme end of the spectrum of intuitiveness, in which case nothing might ever get done if they don't have the *Sensory* around.

Thinking or Feeling?

Here is a question you can ask to figure out which end of the thinking or feeling spectrum the other person is at:

When you're learning something new, do you think about the facts, figures, and other details involved, or do you first wonder how this information will affect other people and their emotions and values?

Both the Thinking and Feeling are important in society. Thinking might get lost in their wonderful world of details but forget about the human element. This is where the Feeling comes into balance the equation, especially in such industries that involve caregiving.

Judging or Perceiving?

To figure out which category someone prefers, simply ask them, Would you rather make lists and plan ahead, or do you prefer to keep things loose and surprise yourself?

Are you stressed out by waiting till the last minute to do things?

The J and the P are valuable in society, whether at work or at home. A great way to maintain balance is to make sure there are always plans and those plans are executed, and then that there's room for optimization. This way, the Judging can get their planning done and feel at ease knowing they've covered all bases, while the Perceiving can get involved in the optimization process where they can see new angles or ways of doing things.

If you understand the way the core of the Myers-Briggs personalities, or any other classification of personalities, work then you should have no problem crafting the right questions to figure out where people stand.

The ability to speed read people is essential. This is how you can make sure there's peace at home and that at work, things are running as they should. It's a great way to build the right sort of friendships and partnerships because you can cut through all the clutter and connect with them on a genuine level.

Common Mistakes When Reading People

Reading people isn't just about asking those questions, although those are helpful. It's also about studying body language. However, not everyone gets that right. Here are common mistakes:

- Not paying attention to the context. Maybe their lips are pressed together only because they're dry. Maybe they have their arms wrapped around their chest because it's cold.

Notice the context before you decide how someone is feeling or what they're thinking.

• Not looking out for clusters. You can't just say someone is lying because they looked up and to the left or whatever. Life is not a poker game. Often, a combination of actions let you know what's going on with someone. Look at these behaviors in clusters, not singles.

• Not figuring out the baseline behavior. If someone blinks a lot when they speak, naturally, but they're suddenly not blinking, that should tell you something is off. Maybe they're lying, or they're holding back, or they're afraid, or they're excited, or something. If you're not sure what it is, then you should see error number one. Pay attention to context.

• Not being aware of your biases. When you don't like someone, it will make you judge them unfairly. Also, when people compliment you, it will affect the way you see them, even if it's on an unconscious level. You must be very neutral when you're attempting to read someone because some people will attempt to make you see them in a different light than they truly are. Whether that is intentional is another matter up for debate.

Chapter Five: How to Read Body Language

Communication doesn't just happen with words. It's in the stuff you don't say. If you will have fulfilling relationships in your personal and professional life, then you've got to learn to communicate. What this means is it's not enough to speak the same language. You've got to pay attention to such things as tone, facial expression, and body language. You've got to pay attention to nonverbal communication.

Why does nonverbal communication matter so much? Because often, body language is the most accurate depiction of what's going on in a person's mind. It's all about various expressions, mannerisms, and other forms of physical behavior that take the words being spoken and wrap them up in a rich tapestry of meaning.

We all know nonverbal communication, some more than others, of course. You could converse with someone and feel something's off about them. You probably were picking up on nonverbal cues, like eye contact, vocal tone, hand gestures, body posture, and so on. Knowing how your body talks is a useful skill because you can detect who's genuine and who's not. You can also communicate so it fosters trust, openness, mutual respect, and bonding. Even when you're silent, you'll know how to be. Trust me when I say even in your silence, your body speaks loudly.

When the words you speak and your body language do not match each other, there is a lack of congruence between the two, and you can seem dishonest. In such situations, people will often go with what they noticed, not what you said, since there's no truer language than your body's.

Why Nonverbal Communication Matters

To know the relevance of nonverbal communication, consider the roles it plays. First, when you're honest, it helps to strengthen whatever message it is you're passing across verbally.

When someone's lying, body language can be immensely helpful. Often, it will contradict the words coming out of their mouth, so you know to take them with a pinch of salt.

When you don't feel like talking, or you're where speaking would not be ideal, body language can save the day. Your expression and the posture you've adopted can help folks figure out what's going on with you, sometimes even better than words could.

Nonverbal communication acts as a wonderful complement to whatever you're saying. For instance, if your colleague were to say, "Hey, great job on that presentation!" You'd love that, naturally. But, if they said that, and gave you a literal pat on the back, that would make you feel even better, as it communicates even stronger the sincerity of their compliment and adoration for you. That's how awesome nonverbal communication is. It can strengthen or underscore the message you're passing across.

Forms of Nonverbal Communication

Posture and body movement can communicate a lot about you at first glance. Posture isn't necessarily about whether you always walk with your head held high and shoulders back because you went to some finishing school. It's more about the carriage. The way you hold your head, sit, walk, and stand. It's the way you move and all the subtle movements you make, which are very telling about you.

Facial expressions are another form of verbal communication - often more expressive than body language since you can communicate quite a range of emotions and messages with your face alone. The great thing about facial expressions is that they're universal, remaining the same no matter the culture.

Eye contact is another key form of nonverbal communication. Sustained eye contact, too little eye contact, or constantly broken eye contact all say various things. Your eyes can show disdain, interest, love, hate, affection, confusion, determination, and so much more. Eye contact is also a great way to determine whether you want to keep engaging someone in conversation or set them free already.

Gestures are unavoidable in everyday life. We point, wave, make the "hang loose" sign, flip someone the bird, slice the air with our hands, and all without thinking too much about it. Some gestures are the same all over the world. Some aren't. I'd be wary of making the OK sign in Brazil, Russia, Germany. Please don't do it.

Space is an interesting form of nonverbal communication. Some people have no concept of personal space. Sometimes, that's a cultural thing. Other times it's simply an inability to read the room. You may have had an experience in which someone was a little too far into in your space, and you felt extremely uncomfortable. Or amazingly comfortable, depending on who they are. With space, you can communicate intimacy, dominance, aggression, or affection.

Touch is another potent nonverbal communication. Think about that clammy, limp hand you once shook. Think about the other hand you shook - the firm, warm one. See how both handshakes most likely affected your perception of the other person? Touch communicates whether it's a stroke on the cheek, a hug, a grip on the arm, or an annoying pat on the head.

Voice is key in communication. It's not just about the words, but the way the words flow from you. You can read people's voices and get more meaning from them than what they're saying. The timing of their speech, pacing, volume, inflection, and tone can say a lot about what the other person is feeling.

Reading Body Language

When you're chatting with someone or addressing a group, here are things to look out for to let you know that the other party is at ease and interested in the conversation:

1. Eye contact is key. Too much can be bad as too little. You want just enough eye contact. If they engage with you visually for many seconds each time, then you have an interested audience. When someone is lying to you, they will often avoid holding your gaze. However, if someone makes a habit of lying, they will deliberately hold your gaze for longer to fix that problem. So, if you notice that someone is holding your gaze too long and too intensely, then they're probably not being honest. Another thing about prolonged eye contact is that it could be threatening, so remember that.

2. Body posture will let you know if they're interested or not. When they stand or sit in an erect position, and they take up a lot of physical space with their body, it means authority and power. It means they're very vested in the conversation. When speaking with someone, if you notice they've crossed their legs or their arms, they might not actually be interested in what you have to say. Be mindful of context, though. Maybe it's cold, so they've crossed their arms. Maybe they always look like they stepped out of a GQ magazine and naturally cross their legs like they're posing for a photo.

3. Genuine smiles are a plus. It's easy to fake a smile, so it seems like all is well, but you can tell when they're forcing it. With a real smile, the eyes crinkle at the corner, showing a pattern that looks like a crow's feet (it's literally called "crow's feet"). This is how you know they do love talking with you.

4. The firmness of a handshake lets you know if this person wants to engage. If it's a firm grip, they're confident and poised. If it's weak, they may be nervous, or they may be secretly contemptuous, or

uninterested. Remember that a very firm handshake could be a subtle sign of aggression.

5. Physical closeness will let you know how comfortable the other person is with you around. If they stand or sit close, then you know they're okay with being there. If they keep their distance, they either don't want to be there because they have something to do, or because they find being with you uncomfortable. This distance between people communicating with each other is known as proxemics, thanks to Edward T. Hall, an anthropologist. He says there are four levels of social distance: 6 to 8 inches shows a close, comfortable relationship, where both parties can hug, touch, whisper, and share any intimate actions. This is an intimate distance. 1.5 to 4 feet is the personal distance, where there are family members or good friends. Social distance is 4 to 12 feet, and this is the space acquaintances or coworkers will often have between each other. Public distance is 12 to 25 feet. This is the space you get between a speaker and their audience at a public speaking event.

6. Too much nodding is not good. They either want you to shut up already so they can get their two cents in, or they don't feel confident being with you. They might be nervous about what you think of them.

7. Are their brows furrowed? If they've got wrinkles in their forehead, and their eyebrows are trying to meet each other, then it means they're either feeling uneasy, or they're confused.

8. Fidgeting means that they're likely nervous, disinterested, or bored. It's when they make a lot of small, unnecessary hand movements, move around in their seat, keep touching their clothes or hair, or other things nearby. Be mindful of context again, as some people like to fidget with things while they think. It might not necessarily mean they're nervous or bored.

More Tips for Reading Nonverbal Communication

Blinking is a natural thing. Some people blink more than others, however, there is still much to learn from nonverbal cue. When people blink too fast, they're probably uncomfortable or in distress. When someone barely blinks, then that's probably a sign they're doing their best to control their eye movements.

Pupil size is an admittedly subtle way to read someone, but still valid. Remember that light in the room can affect the size of the pupils. With that out of the way, it's possible for emotions to cause little changes in pupil size. Say someone's attracted to you. Chances are they're giving you "bedroom eyes," in that their pupils dilate.

The mouth speaks in more ways than one. Besides the words, you can tell a lot from a person's mouth. Are they biting or chewing their bottom lip? Then they may feel insecure, worried, or afraid. If they're biting said bottom lip while giving you a meaningful, flirty look as they hold your eyes, well, there's no worry or fear in what they're communicating. When they cover their mouth, they're probably covering a yawn or a cough, or maybe they're trying to disguise their disapproval.

If they're smiling, then there are lots of things that could be going on, from genuine joy to false happiness, cynicism, and sarcasm. Notice their lips: Are they pursed? Then they might be disapproving of you, find you, or what you're saying distasteful, or they may be disapproving. If their lips are turned up, then they're feeling happy. If they're turned down, they may be sad, or they may not approve. It could also be a pure grimace.

Gestures like a clenched fist could either be a show of solidarity or anger. A thumbs-up signal means approval, while the thumbs down mean disapproval. The V sign, where your middle and index finger are lifted and separated, means victory or peace. If you're in Australia or the UK, it's offensive. The OK gesture, where your thumb and index finger touch to form a circle while the other three fingers are extended, means "alright" or "okay." There are parts of Europe where it means, "you are nothing." If you use it in South American countries, then it carries a vulgar meaning.

Legs and arms matter. Crossed arms mean they're feeling defensive. Crossed legs away from you mean they don't like you, or they're not comfortable with you. Spread arms that take up more room is confident, as they're unconsciously making themselves seem larger, and by extension, more commanding. On the flip side, arms tucked close to their body is a way to keep attention off themselves or an indication they feel small or threatened. Standing with both hands on the hips could be a sign they feel aggressive, or that they're in control. Hands clasped behind the back could mean anger, boredom, or anxiety. Fidgeting or fingers that tap rapidly could mean frustration, boredom, or impatience. Crossed legs could mean they would like some privacy, or they are closed off from you.

Sitting up straight means they are paying attention. If they're hunched forwards, then they're either indifferent or bored. A closed posture where they hide their trunk, cross arms and legs, could mean they're not feeling friendly, or they're hostile, or anxious. When they have an open posture, they keep the body's trunk exposed, showing they are open, eager, willing, and friendly.

Chapter Six: How to Analyze Handwriting

Just like your body talks, so does your handwriting. Big whoop, right? It's just words on paper. No, it's a lot more than the words you write down. Your handwriting can be a dead giveaway of how you felt in the moment you were writing it, or how you are in general. It can offer a baseline for figuring out your personality, feelings, character, and intentions. The science of analyzing handwriting is known as graphology.

Things to Keep in Mind about Graphology

1. Take it with a pinch of salt. Don't assume someone is a crook just because they've got crooked writing. Graphologists say they can find your personality in your handwriting. This is true, but only to a certain extent. You need to also recall you're not an actual expert on graphology, and there are a lot of other things going on with handwriting which graphologists consider before passing judgment on people based on their writing. Please don't judge people based on their handwriting alone. If you do, stay away from doctors, since they are legendary with their illegible handwriting. See? Doesn't make any sense.

2. You will need a proper writing sample. This would ideally be some cursive writing on unlined paper. Remember, though, that not everyone learned to write cursive, so don't assume they're a psycho for writing straight with no frills. If you want to analyze someone's handwriting, you will need more than one sample. Get a few, making sure each was written hours apart. The thing about handwriting is that it changes depending on the mood and circumstance. Having several samples will help you get a baseline for what their handwriting is like.

3. Notice the pressure of the writing strokes. Some folks press hard as they write so that if you were blind, you could probably read it all by just feeling it. Others write lightly. You can tell because the marks on the paper will be a lot lighter, and you might not even feel anything on the other side. According to graphologists, the "hard pressers" are the ones who have high energy, emotionally. It could mean they are sensual, intense, or vigorous. The "average pressers" are supposedly calm and grounded. They have great memory skills and great perception. The "light pressers" are supposedly introverts or those who vibe with low energy.

4. Notice the slant of the writing strokes. When it comes to cursive most folks will write with a slant to one side or the other. You can focus on the letters that have hoops on top, like, h, b, and d to figure out which sort of "slanter" you're dealing with. The "right slanters" are those who are happy to write, and they write fast and with energy. According to graphologists, this means they are confident and assertive. The "left slanter" is not willing to write or is hiding their emotions. According to graphologists, these writers don't cooperate as well as those who slant right. A "no slant" writer apparently has their emotions in control. However, these points may not necessarily apply to people who are left-handed.

5. Check out the baseline of the handwriting. Besides collecting several samples, you will need to go a step further by making sure they're not written on lined sheets. Often, folks won't write in a straight line if there are no lines on the paper. Using a ruler-straight across your collection of handwriting samples, you can compare the angle of

each written sentence. According to graphologists, writing upward shows a happy, upbeat, optimistic mood. Writing downward could mean fatigue or plain discouragement. If the writing is wavy, meaning up and down, it could mean the writer is uncertain, unstable, or unskilled.

6. Notice the letter sizes. When the writer uses small letters, it might mean they are introverted, reclusive, or thrifty. Large letters imply an outgoing, friendly, and extroverted nature.

7. Look at the space between words and letters. If the handwriting makes use of all the space it can, keeping things close together, then graphologists say the writer could be introverted or conscious about themselves. If they drag out the letters, it means they're independent and generous. As for the gaps between words, the closer they are, the more the writer likes crowds. Larger gaps apparently mean they have organized and clear thoughts.

8. Pay attention to the way the letters connect. Graphologists are of the opinion there is a wealth of information to be gleaned from the way a writer connects their letters. The trouble is, there are so many ways people write cursive, so it's hard to conclude on that. However, here are things which graphologists say: Writers who use garlands (curves shaped like cups, open on the top) are warm and strong; writers who use downward curves or arcades are more likely creative since these curves are dignified and slower to write; and writers who use threads, where the pen stroke gets increasingly lighter toward the word's end, or where there are trailing dots, are supposedly rushed and sloppy.

Another Way to Analyze Handwriting

Graphology isn't the only way to study handwriting. You can also make use of forensic document analysis, which is often mistaken for graphology. With this method, you can sometimes get hints about the person's sex, age, and other things like that, but it's not about figuring out their personality. What it's used for is to figure out forgery cases and compare handwriting with things like ransom notes or other evidence.

You must get all the samples you need voluntarily, with the same ink and the same paper. When you're practicing your analysis, you'll need your friends to write out the same, long text. Let them write it at least two times on two pieces of paper. When you're done collecting them, shuffle them together, and then you can go ahead with the methods that follow to match each pair accurately.

Forensic Document Analysis in Practice

1. Criminal investigators will use no less than three samples when dealing with a full letter, or they will use over 20 samples if they're working with a signature. Do the same.

2. Begin by looking for the differences among the letters. It's often a rookie mistake to start off looking for similarities, and then assume that it's the same writer without carrying out any further investigation. So, your first task is to look for all how the letters are different before you move on to looking for similarities.

3. Check out the baseline alignment by using the paper's line or a ruler under the writing when working with unlined paper. Some writers write below the line, while others write above. Some keep it level throughout, while others are up and down.

4. Track the space between each letter. This is the most objective way to make your comparisons. You'll need a ruler with a millimeter measure so that you can measure how much space is between words and letters. If there's a lot of difference in the spacing, then it could mean different writers. This is more than likely the case if there's one writing sample where the words are connected with strokes of the pen, and another sample has gaps.

5. Notice the relationship in height between the letters. Does the writer have a habit of writing their cursive Ks or Ls above the other letters, or are they the same height? Often, this is a gauge much better than the loop width and letter slant.

6. Now, it's time to compare the shapes of the letter. There are lots of connectors, loops, curves, and letter endings that allow you to tell writers apart. The long and short of it is, you must check out a long piece of writing, and then compare that with a sample by someone else. First, look for the various versions of a letter in a single sample, so you can see what differences you can't rely on. No one writes the same way in the same document throughout. This way, you can rule out what you can't use. Next, look for a letter pretty much the same each time it shows up. People who write in cursive script will often either use the cursive version of the letter, a single, vertical stroke, or they will use that stroke but add in crossbars at the bottom and the top.

7. If you're feeling like Sherlock, you could deliberately seek signs of forgery by getting your friends to sign someone else's signature, and then put them all in a pile along with the original. Here are things to know with forgeries: Because the forger has to write slowly to copy the signature properly, there might be tremors and inconsistency in the thickness of the lines. Real signatures will have a change in line thickness as you speed up and slow down when you sign stuff. Also, look out for pen lifts (little gaps that appear in the signature) and inkblots, which naturally happen because the forger pauses or hesitates. You can find them at the beginning and end of the forged signature, or even between the letters. Also, attempt to sign your own signature no less than five times. You'll notice that it varies each time. If you notice there are two signatures too similar, matching every line and curve, then chances are one of them is the forgery.

Fun Graphology Facts

1. How high you put the bar in the letter "t" tells a lot about you. When the bar on the letter "t" is above the letters that precede and follow it, it shows that you're optimistic. This is especially the case when the bar also has an upward slant to it. It means you're the person who reaches for your goal, no matter what. A low T-bar is not a good

thing, especially if it is lower than the preceding and following letters. It means you underestimate your abilities, and you have no belief in yourself. You have low self-esteem, according to graphologists. If you have a downward slant to the T-bar, then that's even worse because it means you're depressed, according to Mike Mandel, graphologist, and hypnotist.

2. Lower zones are very telling. These are where the loops in a word go down and below the letters. Think of the small letter g, or y, for instance. According to Mike Mandel, the bigger the loop is, the more friends you need. The smaller the loop, the less you need friends in your life. The person who writes a g without a loop is really not even interested in close friends. They might have one, or none, and that's about it for them. They're okay with going it all alone when they need to. The bigger loop writer will need more people, or they cannot cope.

3. The size of your loop can reveal your sexual appetite. Again, those with large loops have a strong and healthy sexual appetite. They have a desire for stuff, money, food, and good things in life. Some don't have a loop when they write, but instead will draw the line straight down to a defined point, and then a curved hook back to the left. According to Mike Mandel, this is called the felon's claw. This appears in the handwriting of no less than 80 percent of felons in the American penitentiary system. Mandel says the felon's claw is a sure sign of manipulation and is a dangerous sign.

4. Graphologists do not judge people based on single letters or a pen slip. That's not enough to label them sane or psychotic. You also cannot judge them by stuff they've written on a board with chalk or a marker. They study people based on their usual handwriting, preferably written while they're sitting down, comfortable, writing on an unlined sheet of paper, and their preferred pencil or pen. The goal is to get them to write so it mirrors, as close as possible, their usual method of writing.

5. "Weird handwriting equals weird people; weird lower zones, really weird person," says Mike Mandel. You have the felon's claw, but

when the lower zone is something particularly weird, maybe with several weird loops, then you're dealing with someone with weird sex drives and sexual deviation to the most extreme degrees.

6. The signature you have is the personality you give the world, not your actual personality. It's not you. So, when you're going into a business or personal relationship with somebody, you want to know that their handwriting and their signature look similar. If they seem the same, that means this person is a straight shooter, and what you see is what you get when you deal with them. If the handwriting is legible, but the signature is just odd, and all over the place, they're holding something back about themselves and are not honest about who they are. It could be out of self-defense.

7. Signatures can let you know if a marriage is on the rocks. When a woman marries a man and takes on his last name, the space she puts between her first name and his last name shows how close or far apart they are in her mind.

8. A signature can also let you know if there's a problem between the writer and their family. If they sign with their first and last name, and they cross out their last name, they might justify it as a style or say that's how they've always crossed written it. However, on an unconscious level, they've crossed it out because they have no connection with their family or wish to distance themselves from their father or mother or some other relatives. Basically, they don't connect with their loved ones, according to Mike Mandel.

With proper training in graphology, you can learn the fascinating things about people based on their handwriting alone, and it could almost make you seem like you're psychic. But! There's no woo-woo going on here. It's all down to pure science and research.

Why Reading Handwriting is a Useful Skill

It would save us all so much trouble if we could figure out who people were based on thought bubbles that appeared on top of their heads. Imagine you knew everything someone was about, right from the get-go. You'd know whether you want to date them, so you'd never have to deal with needless heartbreak. You would know whether to trust a teenager to babysit your child or if you'd be better off taking them with you to work and risk annoying your boss and coworkers.

If you knew right from the start who you were dealing with, then you would know whether to lend them that money, or whether you want to enter into a business relationship with them. Sadly, there's no way to peer into the essence of someone (other than the eyes, perhaps). Therefore, you need to rely on *not just what they say*, but nonverbal cues and other things like handwriting.

When you have the professional knowledge that expert graphologists do, it can become a lot easier for you to figure out who you're dealing with. Again, I'm not suggesting you cancel someone based on the information you get from this book. I am saying, however, that you would be more cautious of who you're dealing with, and you probably would save yourself lost dollars and lost time.

Handwriting analysis can be useful when trying to figure out who to hire for a certain job, so you know you're going with the person who is likely to be more productive and less of a headache. It can be useful in understanding the people you're dealing with, and whether it's worth it to get into arguments with them or try to explain things to them. You may know a few people always looking for a fight, no matter what. There's just no reasoning with them. If you had the opportunity to assess their handwriting before engaging with them, and you knew of the science of graphology, you probably have saved yourself a headache or two. That's why handwriting analysis matters. It can help you understand people and make life a lot easier.

Chapter Seven: Mind-Reading with Neuro-Linguistic Programming

If you want to do a stellar job of reading other people's minds, then you should look to neuro-linguistic programming. To understand Neuro-linguistic programming (NLP), let's look at the three basic parts to the term. Neuro is short for neurology and is basically the physical, emotional, and mental aspects of brain function. Linguistic refers to the language you use, and how you engage in communication with others, and even more important, the way you communicate with you. Programming is the way your past thoughts, emotions, and experiences affect every aspect of your life. So, to summarize, NLP is the language of your mind.

NLP in Action

There are three key elements in NLP:
- Modeling
- Action
- Effective communication

If someone can figure out how someone else finishes their tasks, then they can copy that process, and they can also let others know how to finish those tasks.

Everyone has a view of reality that is personal. NLP practitioners will critically analyze their perspectives, and others' perspectives so that they can have a holistic view of an event or situation. Once you can grasp the variations in perspectives, you gain valuable information. There is no better way to learn this information than by taking advantage of your mind and body, immersing yourself in these experiences.

NLP Mind Reading

The process of NLP's mind-reading involves assuming that you're well aware of what someone else feels or thinks in any particular situation. The truth is no one could ever know the entirety of your thoughts and emotions. They may have a close match, but not the full picture. So, if you have ever felt certain you know how someone feels or what they're thinking, then you're mind-reading –a tricky thing that can get you into trouble.

In reading minds, you must account for the parts of the other person's experience which you can actually verify with your own senses. Once you assume you know every little thought in their head, then you forget that thought you know it all is actually your thought, and not necessarily a reflection of objective reality.

How to Mind Read

Sometimes, we believe we know what other people's intentions are based on the way they act or don't act. We could assume that someone is really into us, or that they're not, or that they're out to get us. Reading minds with NLP reveals that "the map is not the territory," as one NLP presupposition says. We've all made mistakes when it comes to jumping to conclusions about the way others feel or about why they chose to do certain things. With ourselves, we judge based on intention. With others, we judge based on actions.

We also forget that no one is a mind reader in the *actual sense of the term*. We somehow expect our significant other to know without using our words that we're mad because they forgot to take the trash out again, or that we appreciate the amazing dinner they put together. This can cause a lot of trouble, because if both parties expect the other to somehow always know what's on their mind without checking in, then there's a lot of room for misunderstanding.

How CAN You Read People's Minds?

We need to discuss accessing cues. When people are thinking about something, they often will show some subtle action that lets them activate the right representation of what they're thinking. They might move their eyes, change their position, breathe differently, make certain gestures, change their intonation, and so on.

These behaviors are useful cues you can keep track of, so you know how they might be about to respond to an event or to you. These cues won't tell you the meat of what they're thinking, but it will let you know *how* they think.

For instance, if you've ever seen someone who's making faces, scratching an itch, out of breath, using onomatopoeic sounds, or making familiar hand gestures, you may not ascribe any meaning to these actions all on their own. However, you can tell what actual process is going on with their mind when they do these things.

As you practice NLP, you will decipher these behaviors easily, and this will put you in a position to affect the way others think. Here are patterns which you should know:

1. Auditory mode accessing cues: Here, the eyes and head lean sideways, all gestures happen at ear level, and the breathing is diaphragmatic. The speed of their speech will switch between fast and slow, and their intonation will go up and down.

2. Kinesthetic mode accessing cues: Here, the eyes and head are down. All gestures are directed to the body, and the breathing is down in the belly. Their speech gets slower, and their intonation goes deeper.

3. Visual mode accessing cues: Here, the eyes and head are up. All gestures will be made upward, or above the shoulders. They breathe in the upper part of the respiratory system (the lungs), and their eyes are halfway closed. Also, the voice goes higher in pitch and speed.

Practice Accessing Cues

You're going to need a friend for this one! When you're done, have them let you know what you did after each step. You want them to pay attention to what happened with your facial expression, posture, gestures, breathing, and tone of voice.

1. Recall something fun you did or were a part of.

2. Pay attention to the physical sensations you had from that experience.

3. Now, let the feelings go.

4. Next, think about the pictures tied to your experience.

5. Now, let the pictures go.

6. Next, pay attention to the sounds tied to your experience.

7. Now, let the sounds go.

Now, time to switch places.

Who Uses NLP?

NLP is used in self-help and therapy circles, and in complicated ways such as AI banking technology to discover whether people who have never taken a loan or even owned a bank account are likely to make good on their debts. It's that amazing.

In NLP, the map is not the territory because it often will show you the stark differences between reality and belief. Each person will act based on their perspective of things, not pure objectivity. There are as many maps as there are people. So, it's the NLP therapists' job to figure out what your map is like, and the way this map may affect your thoughts and actions.

The therapist uses NLP to help people figure out their behavioral and thinking patterns, aspirations, and emotional state. Armed with this information, they can help their patients to do better at the skills that benefit them and develop ways of dropping the habits that are unproductive.

Hypnotic Mind Reading Techniques

1. The Delayed Echo: Most people enjoy talking about themselves, and as they do, you invariably learn something about them. You learn things like the name of their cousin's cat, what they did in Cape Town during the summer, and all sorts of other info. Often, they mention them in passing, so they eventually forget they did mention it. Here's where you get to "read minds" by paying close attention. What must you do? Remember every fact. Do your best not to draw their attention to the information they shared. Right away, talk about anything else besides that bit of info. Give it about five minutes, when they must have forgotten what they told you. Finally, mention the cat or holiday experiences, but use different phrases and words from the ones they used to share that info with you. This way, you're literally their delayed echo. As you use different language, you seem like you somehow picked up on their experiences, like you had a crystal ball or something.

2. Flattery: People find it flattering when you can see them for who they are on the inside. As you describe them, your description might not be accurate, but often those traits you're talking about will be relatable and easy to identify with. Am I advocating you lie to someone about them? No. It matters that your flattery is strictly founded upon truth. This is not only honest, but the listener is also likely to believe you because of it. I will give a few examples here, but please remember that they work particularly with Western culture. When dealing with people from other cultures, they might not work –

or be acceptable. General traits you can assume of someone include friendliness, hard-working, smart, positive, reliable, resourceful, loyal, and honest. Traits you can assume are true of females are helpful, perceptive, underappreciated, intuitive, sensitive. As for males, you can assume their traits include, rational, independent, confident, excellent problem-solving skills, practical.

3. Covering All Possibilities (CAP): This "mind-reading technique" is like the previous one, except you pick two opposing traits. You want to make sure you choose general traits, not facts that can be quantified and thus disproven. For instance, you could say, "You love to hear people out, but sometimes you can get a bit impatient." This general statement could apply to anyone. They will be accepting of it because you've first highlighted the positive side to them, which takes the sting out of your negative observation. Therefore, a lot of horoscope readings seem to be oh so accurate. In making these statements, you might want to add humor to make it even easier for the listener to accept.

4. The Barnum Effect: This is named after the famous circus leader, PT Barnum. Here, you make a very specific statement, yet, it's one that could apply to almost anyone. You begin by making a general statement, and then you observe their reaction. Based on this reaction, you can move on to more specific statements. Here's how that would work: "You're a kind person — [wait for reaction] — no matter how bad things turn out; you always look for the best in the experience. You tend to find opportunities where others don't and make the best of what you've got." Now, let's try this again, but with the presumption that the reaction is negative: "You're not afraid to dream — [wait for reaction] — but you're also very practical. You don't let your dreams remain dreams. You love to root everything you do firmly in reality, and that's why you'll go places." If you're very astute, you'll notice those examples used both the flattery method and the CAP method. Now, you want to make sure you also use negative personality traits when describing them, so you don't appear to be pandering or making absurd leaps. You could start off saying, "You tend to be hard on yourself," or "You're quite talented at keeping grudges indefinitely," or "There are things you've done in the past that you regret deeply."

5. The Seven Ages of Man: This is also called "universal experiences." With this technique, you're leaning heavily on the things we've all gone through at various points in our lives. Basically, you seek what people may be going through at the moment based on their age. Remember that the examples to follow are based on Western culture. Sometimes, certain examples are considered out of style, so you want to remember that . Here are the seven ages of man:

18 to 22: At this time, you leave home, and you explore many lifestyles. You want to prove that you can make it in the world of adults.

22 to 30: You're either off seeking an adventure or building a nest. You're either avoiding commitment or actively seeking it out. Also, career matters a lot.

30 to 35: You're re-evaluating everything you've done with life. If you were all about adventure, you think of settling down. If you were all about building a nest, you wonder what your commitments may be keeping you from.

33 to 45: The infamous midlife crises. You either finally break away from your commitments to seek new adventures, or you finally settle down to have the family you've been running away from. You feel, erroneously, that you're running out of time and that life is passing you by, so you want to make the most of it.

45 to 55: Your career is wrapping up. It all comes down to how well you handle your midlife crises. If you did well, then that means you'll have experienced a wonderful rebirth. If not, you'll feel like there's no hope, and you'd be disappointed in yourself.

55 to 75: You're done with work. Now you have more time, resources, and freedom to travel, explore, and have fun. You

have fewer responsibilities. However, health might become an issue. Your friends pass on, and you start feeling lonely.

Armed with these facts, you can get backdoor access to someone's thoughts. You may not totally know their age, but you can make a rough estimate and read them based on that.

Chapter Eight: Dark Psychology — Recognizing the Dark Triad

"Some men just want to watch the world burn." Remember that quote by Alfred Pennyworth? Well, it's spot on. There are those who are downright difficult to live with, no matter what you do. They might be arrogant, with a penchant for being mercurial and domineering, but you can work with them to help them improve focusing on their strengths and neutralizing the less-than-desirable traits they have.

However, there's this other class of people who live only for the view of a world set on fire. They have toxic, damaging behaviors, poisoning and destroying those around them, in every way possible. These people's three traits are the sole components of the "Dark Triad," a term coined by psychologists. Here are the traits:

- Narcissism
- Machiavellianism
- Psychopathy

Now let's describe each one as best we can.

Narcissism: The word "narcissism" is from Greek mythology. There was a hunter named Narcissus, who had fallen deeply in love with his reflection, which he'd spotted by chance in a pool of water. He fell so deeply in love he fell into the water and drowned.

Narcissists are selfish, lacking in empathy, arrogant, boastful, and overly sensitive to criticism.

Machiavellianism: This world exists thanks to Niccolo Machiavelli, an Italian politician and diplomat from the 16th century. He wrote a book called "The Prince" in 1513, and it was basically awash with praise for deceit and cunning in diplomatic matters. Machiavellian traits include manipulation, duplicity, self-interest, and a lack of morality and emotion.

Psychopathy: The traits of psychopathy include antisocial behavior, lack of remorse and empathy, and being volatile and manipulative. Remember that there's a difference between being an actual psychopath and simply having psychopathic traits. Often, psychopaths engage in criminal violence.

All these personalities are incredibly difficult to read. The narcissist, for instance, has mastered the art of seeming sincere and true when needed. They're a master at reflecting whatever you want to see. So how do you spot these people?

How to Spot Your Neighborhood Narcissist

The narcissist oozes charm like no one else. A study showed that you could only see through their smoke and mirrors by the seventh time you meet them. Falling in love with them can ruin you. Literally, they will take a greatly confident person with high self-esteem and turn them into unrecognizable versions of themselves. Here are the hallmarks of Narcissistic Personality Disorder:

1. A grand sense of self-importance, where they overhype their talents, skills, and achievements. The narcissist wants you to know how awesome they are. If they haven't actually achieved anything yet, they will brag to you about how they're going to. They need to be constantly appreciated, recognized, and validated.

2. Dreams and aspirations of unlimited success, power, beauty, brilliance, or "ideal" love.

3. A need for constant, excess admiration. As for the narcissist, their job is to talk about themselves, and your job is to listen. They won't ask about you. When you do chip in something about your own life, they're quick to turn the spotlight back on themselves. This can quickly get annoying and boring. On the flip side, narcissists are masters of charm. They're successful, beautiful, or talented, and these are things that keep us all enamored with them. However, those narcissists are great at the art of seduction and can make you feel greatly loved and admired. Until they're bored.

4. A belief they are unique and special and can only be understood by those who are unique or special; in other words, people they perceive to be of high status. They also believe they should only ever associate with these "special" people (or organizations.) This is why they'll name-drop, only patronize the best restaurants, and have the most expensive toys. It's all just to hide how empty they are inside.

5. A lack of empathy for other people's emotions and needs. There are people who lack empathy but aren't narcissists. However, this trait is essential when identifying the narcissist in your midst. Pay attention to their face and body language when you recount a sad story. They can be rude, refuse to listen to you, decide for you without seeking your input, and so on. These are only little things but put all these actions together, and you'll notice you might be dealing with a narc.

6. A sense of entitlement to special treatment and constant compliance with their every wish. As far as they're concerned, the world revolves around them. If it doesn't, then someone had better fix it. They don't think the rules apply to them. Nothing is ever their fault.

7. A tendency to take advantage of people and exploit them to get their own personal gains. They take and take, but they don't give. When they do, there's a motive.

8. A belief that others envy them, and never-ending of clothes they perceive, is doing better than they are.

9. An air of arrogance.

How to Spot Your Master Machiavellian

To summarize the personality of the Machiavellian, you only need to look at two quotes from the book, The Prince. "A wise ruler ought never to keep faith when, by doing so, it would be against his interests." How about this other lovely little gem: "A prince never lacks good reasons to break his promise."? Machiavellian believes that honesty is not needed if it would make more sense to use force, deceit, and treachery instead.

The Machiavellian is a master manipulator. They are duplicitous, constantly deceiving people to get what they want. They have no sense of morals and consider other people nothing more than steppingstones to get where they need to. The Machiavellian believes that anyone who allows themselves to be used most likely deserved it.

Sure, we can all be dishonest every now and then, but for the Machiavellian, this is just another Tuesday. The "High Mach" sincerely believes in this quote by Groucho Marx, "Sincerity is everything. If you can fake that, you've got it made." It was only a joke, but don't tell the High Mach that. Here are five traits you can spot them by:

1. The High Mach does best in social situations and careers where the rules are not set in stone, allowing them to get creative with boundaries.

2. For the High Mach, holding a cynical outlook on life and being emotionally detached helps them to keep their impulses in check, and teaches them to be patient in their opportunism.

3. The High Mach believes in using such tactics as guilt, charm, self-disclosure, friendliness, and, when needed, pressure. Anything to get their way.

4. The High Mach would much rather be subtle about their tactics. They masquerade as being friendly, they pour on the charm, make you feel guilty, and share stuff with you about themselves when they must, to give you a false sense of solidarity. This way, they can conceal their actual intentions and give themselves room for plausible

deniability if you catch them at their game. They're not above pressure and threats when needed.

5. Most people would rather have the High Mach on their side with negotiations, debates, and other competitive situations. However, no one wants to have them as colleagues, friends, or spouses.

How to Spot Your Sadistic Psychopath

This is the psychopath, summed up in a Ted Bundy quote: "I don't feel guilty for anything. I feel sorry for people who feel guilt." Fortunately, for most of us, we need not deal with psychopaths in our everyday lives. However, if you have to, it helps to know the person you're dealing with. Here are various traits noticeable in this personality:

1. Manipulation is considered "high art" to them. Perhaps the psychopath is the grandmaster of manipulation. They know how to suck you into their lies, make you see what they want you to see, and nothing more. Even when you know the truth, and it niggles at you in the back of your mind, they know how to make you desperate to believe their version of events.

2. They are experts at reading people. The psychopath has an uncanny ability to size you up in just an instant at your first meeting. They hardly ever get it wrong. Best believe they will explore every weakness about you they can. Somehow, they can home in on your soft spot and take advantage of it. Whether you've got a big heart, or you are all about a big score, a quick and easy win, or you're just gullible, they'll know, and they'll use it. When you're in a personal relationship with a psychopath, they will learn everything about you they can, and then they will turn that knowledge into an arsenal of deadly weapons they expertly wield against you, cutting you down bit by bloody bit, until there's nothing left of you. Sounds dramatic, but that's the psychopath.

3. They are charming. Not that you should be wary of charming people; this just means the psychopath can instantly disarm you with charm. That's their thing. They don't even have to try.

4. They will blindside you with pain. They have all this information on you, but they won't use it right away. They're happy to wait and use it against you in the future when they feel it will deal you the most damage. People are often shocked when the psychopath finally strikes, and the mask comes off.

5. They will say whatever you want to hear. If you've been in a relationship with them for a while, it can be shocking when you learn they've only been using you, telling you what you want to hear. Often family and friends of psychopathic murderers are shocked because they never gave even a hint of evil.

6. They do not have a conscience. They have no moral compass. They're ready to act in whatever ways they please to get what they want, or just to add more fire to the flames. It's not just that they do heinous things. They relish being terrible. There's no rhyme or reason for the joy that they feel in destroying everything around them.

7. They cannot relate to fear. They're incapable of it. They might feel it, but they don't know how to automatically detect it, let alone respond to it.

8. Their work history is inconsistent. You'd be hard-pressed to find them working a job for too long. They might get bored and move on, or they might fire themselves. Whichever the case, they're exceptionally good at explaining away their inconsistency with work that it's easy to believe their stories without further questioning.

9. They have dead, lifeless eyes. A quick Google search for famous psychopaths will show you that. It's almost as if there is no soul behind those eyes. Even when they're upbeat, charming, and seemingly happy, those eyes stay flat.

10. They talk in a monotone voice; you can hardly get them to speak louder. Also, since the psychopath has no actual emotions, their speech doesn't have that natural rise and fall that others have.

11. They have no empathy. They cannot relate to someone else's pain, and they couldn't be bothered to do so. The only emotions they will respond to are extreme displays of fear and anger, and that's only because they want to exploit these emotions, just for kicks.

12. The psychopath is arrogant and entitled. Keep in mind that regardless of their upbringing, whether they grew up privileged or disadvantaged, they all have that sense of entitlement, and everything they do or say comes from that place.

13. The psychopath doesn't care for rules and doesn't play by them. They will blatantly flaunt them, just for the fun of getting away with it to show how they are above it all.

14. When they do get caught, they don't care about the consequences of their actions. They literally treat getting caught as just the cost of doing business. It doesn't stop them from doing more awful things to others.

15. They will lie to your face without pause. They'll weave fantastic tales to draw you in. And you'll let them. You'll buy into it. Not because you're stupid, but because they're skilled liars.

16. As kids, they are usually violent toward their siblings or pets. They kill animals, just for fun. Where the sociopath learns to become that way, the psychopath is born, not made.

17. Finally, the psychopath is all about the fun of controlling others. They love to dominate and have everyone under their thumb. That's all they live for.

The dark triad of narcissism, Machiavellianism, and psychopathy is something we could all do without. You'll find that there is some overlap in traits with these personalities. They can be damaging and toxic with personal relationships, where you're more than likely to let down your guard and let them in.

I read a story about a woman dealing with identity fraud. She's had her bank accounts and credit cards compromised. The one person who supported her through this was her fiancé, who had moved in with her. She was in touch with the FBI in hopes of solving the case.

She had to deal with stress and anxiety, and this got no better as the authorities were having trouble tracking down the culprit.

Her fiancé was a stalwart and staunch support for her in these times. He comforted her. He bought her gifts. He paid the monthly rent for her – from money she'd given him. After months, her landlord came to confront her for not paying her rent for several months in a row. She then realized that her fiancé had been stashing her rent money for himself, using it only to buy her gifts. It was difficult to come to terms with her being in love with a manipulative, gaslighting narcissist.

There are tales even worse than this one. A quick google search will show you countless experiences and encounters people have had with them of the dark triad. This is why it is more important than ever to learn how to spot these people. You cannot read them the way you'd read regular folk, but certain traits will show up often, letting you know to put a lot of distance between you and them.

These people are callous, and you need to protect yourself. Do not reason with them, do not attempt to get them to change, and do not try to win them over. It may seem like you're making progress, but I promise you they're only playing a game with you; you will lose – and lose hard. If you suspect you might be dealing with someone with a dark triad personality, then the first thing to do is seek the help of a professional psychotherapist. Please do not walk up to them to confront them. That would do nothing except put you on their radar or encourage them to move up the timeline of whatever evil they have planned for you.

Please be willing to share your experience with others. It does no good trying to cover it up. That's just one way to deny the validity of your experience, and it does no one any good. You can educate yourself more on these dark triad personalities so that if you meet them, you're well equipped to handle them if you are where you can't avoid them.

Chapter Nine: Signs of Lies and Deception

Everyone can lie. A lot of us do - there's no use denying that. It's been studied, and scientists have found that you're likely to tell a couple of lies a day. If everyone lies, and lies that often, then it becomes important to tell when they do so.

How to go about reading people to see if they're deceitful is to see what they're usually like when they're honest. For instance, if you asked them, "What's your name?" you could use that to observe where they look, how their voice sounds, and how they breathe. You could follow up with similar questions that there's no use lying about, such as where they're from (assuming they have no reason to deny where they're from.)

Once you've got their baseline, you have only to look for changes in facial expressions, bodily movements, the content of speech, and tone of voice. It's not that simple, though. For instance, they may be fidgety, but only because they're nervous, not lying. Their voice may crack, but only out of anxiety, not because they're fibbing. There are lots of reasons they could seem uneasy when they're answering your questions.

Lying Hands

When you're talking to a liar, they will often make hand gestures after they've spoken, instead of before or during their speech. The reason for this is that the mind is working hard to piece together a story, see if the story is being bought, and what they can do to beef it up if it isn't. So, instead of the usual gesture made before or during a statement, you get one that comes after they've spoken.

There was a study carried out by the University of Michigan in 2015, where the researchers considered 120 video clips of high-profile court cases. They wanted to decipher how people act when they're honest, versus when they're lying. They found that the liars would often use both hands to gesture, more often than those being honest. It's worth mentioning that 40 percent of the clips with liars showed them using both hands to gesture, compared to 25 percent of the honest people.

Another remarkable thing about hands and liars is that when they're dishonest, the liars will unconsciously have their palms facing away This signifies that they're not telling you the full story, they're hiding how they feel, or they're flat-out lying. They might put their hands underneath the table and keep them there. They might simply keep them in their pockets.

Itchy and Fidgety

When someone cocks their head to the side, moves their body in rocking back and forth motion, or shuffles their feet, they might be deceiving you about something. As the liar lies, there are fluctuations in their body's autonomic nervous system. The ANS deals with bodily functions and can play a part in giving away the liar. When you're nervous, you will feel fluctuations in your nervous system, interpreting them as tingle or itches, causing you to fidget. There's also research spearheaded by R. Edward Geiselman, a psychology professor at UCLA, which shows that when people are dishonest, they engage in "grooming behaviors." They play with their hair, check underneath their nails for dirt, and things like that.

Giving Face

When someone's lying to you, they might either look away or stare at a critical moment. They move their eyes about because they're trying to come up with something to say. Geiselman's research also found that people tend to look away for a bit when they lie. The 2015 University of Michigan study also found that liars stare a lot more than those who are truthful. Interestingly, 70 percent of the clips they viewed showed the liars staring directly at the people they lied to.

Even with all these studies, there is still room for debate about eye contact and lying. Plos One published a study in 2012 that discredited the idea that people look in a certain direction as they lie. Sure, maybe you might read too much of nothing into someone else's behavior, but you cannot discount the eyes, as they often hold the truth.

When someone is holding back information from you, then they might roll their lips back, so they almost aren't visible. It's often because they're holding back facts or trying to keep their emotions in check.

The UCLA study showed that someone lying to you would often purse their lips when you ask them questions that they find sensitive. The pursed lips say they don't want to talk about the subject at the moment.

Skin complexion also gives liars away. When someone is talking, and they go white or pale, it could mean that they're not truthful, as blood rushes out of their face.

Are they dry or sweaty? The autonomic nervous system will often cause a liar to sweat in their T-area (the forehead, upper lip, chin, and areas around the mouth.) They might also have to contend with dry eyes and a dry mouth. You can tell by observing how often they squint or blink, and whether they swallow hard, or bite or lick their lips.

The Voice Behind the Words

When you're dealing with a nervous person, it's not unusual for the vocal cords to tighten up. This is a natural response to being in a stressful situation, and it causes the voice to become high-pitched. There might also be a creak in their voice. When someone clears their throat in these situations, it could be because they're trying to deal with the uncomfortably tight muscles, and that could also be a sign that they're lying.

If you notice that they've suddenly turned up the volume, maybe they're getting defensive about something. Whether or not this means they're lying depends on the context.

The Words

When someone has to say stuff like, "Let me be honest," "Trust me," "I want to be truthful to you," then they might be working a little too hard to make you think they're honest. Be mindful of judging them based on these phrases, though, as this isn't a hard-and-fast rule.

There's a little something known as "vocal fill" - filler words like "like," "ah," "uh," and "um," among others. It's often a sign of deception. When people talk like this, they might be trying to give themselves more time to come up with a good lie.

Unless you're part of the dark triad of personalities, we're all, mostly, not natural liars. Because of this, we sometimes spill the tea without meaning to. Sometimes, a person might slip up by saying, "I kissed her — no, wait, I mean she kissed me," or "I was on the I-95 as at then — wait, no, I was actually grabbing a bite to eat." You're dealing with someone who doesn't have the best memory – or, you're dealing with a liar.

Do they speak in sentence fragments? If they're not completing their sentences, then they might be spinning a story on the spot.

Tips for Spotting Liars

Notice when they do not refer to themselves in the story. When people are honest, they will often use the pronoun "I" to let you know what they did. "I kicked off my shoes before I unlocked the door and stepped into his house. As I walked in, I noticed a strange-looking man with a greenish pallor seated on the rocking chair to my right. Since it was a bit dark, I didn't notice the weapon in his hand sooner. I felt nothing for a few seconds, and then the pain overwhelmed me. But I was able to fire off a couple of shots at him before I went down." Notice the use of the many pronouns, "I," here.

When people are untruthful, they will often speak in a way that reduces attention to themselves. They speak with the passive voice as they describe what happened. They'll say, "The door was unlocked," rather than "I unlocked the door." They'll say, "the man was shot," rather than "I fired off a couple of shots."

Another way they try to take the attention off themselves is by using the word "you" instead of "I". For instance, if asked, "Can you tell me why you shot him?" they might reply, "You know, you can't really be too careful. You do your best to make sure that no one gets hurt, and sometimes when things are really dangerous, that means you have to take the most extreme course of action."

Sometimes, whether they're recounting the experience in oral or written form, they will omit pronouns. "Took off shoes. The door unlocked, so, walked into the house. Man with green skin and gun sitting on the rocking chair. Boom! Gun goes off."

Notice the verb tense they use. If they're honest, they will use the past tense to describe events. When someone is lying, they often talk about the events like they're happening in the present – a surefire sign that they're rehearsing their lies. As you listen, notice the precise points at which they switch from past tense to present tense.

If they answer your questions with questions, something's up. As I mentioned before, we're not born liars. A liar doesn't want to lie; there's a chance they'll get caught. They might answer your question with a question so they need not provide an answer. If you asked, "Why did you shoot him?" they might ask, "Why would I shoot someone if they weren't a threat?" or, "Do I look like I just go in guns blazing to you?"

Beware of equivocation. If they avoid answering your questions by using vague and uncertain expressions, and weak modifiers, then you want to be on high alert. I'm talking about words like "maybe," "sort of," "think," "perhaps," "guess," "about," "approximately," "could," "might," and so on. These expressions give them some wiggle room to back out of statements they make when confronted in the future.

Also, watch out for noncommittal verbs like "assume," "figure," "believe," "guess," and so on, and vague qualifiers like "more or less," or "you might say."

Oaths are a red flag. The liar will do their best to convince you that what they say is "God's honest truth." You must believe them, because "cross my heart" they'd never lie. You'll hear, "I swear." Sometimes that's not enough, so they'll say, "I swear on my honor," or "I swear on my mother's grave." Conversely, someone who is honest does not feel the need to convince you, since they are confident of what they're saying and certain that the facts will stand up for them.

Euphemisms are also red flags. Almost every language will give an alternate term for most actions and situations. Guilty liars will use vague or mild words, rather than synonyms explicit in nature. They do this to make you listen more favorably and downplay whatever they did. So if they say "missing" when they could have said "stolen," replace the word "took" with "borrowed," say "bumped" rather than "hit," or claim to have "warned" someone instead of saying "threatened," then you're likely dealing with a liar.

A liar will allude to actions. They'll never really say they did them. They'll say, "I try to make sure I water the lawn every day," rather than "I water the lawn every day." Or, "I decided that we were going to take a walk through the woods." Well, did they walk through the woods?" They might say, "I needed to go over the books with her." Did they?

All these are allusions, and they're not saying definitively that they did -or did not - do these things.

Liars will give too little detail. They want to keep their statements short and sweet. Few liars have the imagination to create detailed stories of things that never happened. Besides, the fewer the details, the better for the liar, so they don't get caught when contradicting evidence pops up. Now, when telling the truth, details that seem inconsequential will pop up, because they're trying to pull from long term memory, which stores many things besides this main event. Some liars know this and will go the whole nine yards to craft a lot of detail in their story. Better ones will genuinely convince themselves of these details, accepting them as true, so you have no choice but to read them as honest. These are likely a part of the dark triad.

Pay attention to the narrative balance of their story. When narrating, you have the prologue, the main event, and the epilogue or aftermath. When someone is telling the truth, the prologue will be about ⅕ to ¼ part of the narrative, the main event will be ⅖ to ⅗ of the narrative, and the aftermath will be about ¼ of it all. If these parts feel longer than needed, they may be chock full of lies.

Notice how many words are in a sentence. This is known as the "mean length of utterance" or MLU, which is calculated by adding up the number of words in an entire statement, and then dividing the total by the number of sentences in the statement. Mostly, people speak in sentences of about 10 to 15 words each. When they're anxious, they will speak in sentences noticeably longer or shorter.

Remember: do not focus on body language only. True, there are certain body movements that would allude to the possibility that you're witnessing the birth of a fairy tale, but some of the classic lying cues given by the body aren't tied to lying alone. Sometimes, with the eyes, it's possible that they're only thinking of trying to get to their long-term memory when they look in a "lying direction." This is based on research by psychologist Howard Ehrlichman, who's been studying eye movement since the 1970s. Body language is useful for seeking out lies, but you can't depend on them alone.

Pay attention to the right signals. While there are valid cues for spotting lies, the trouble is these cures can be very weak ways to detect deception. The most accurate cues you should focus on are vagueness, where the speaker is not adding in significant details; vocal uncertainty, where they seem unsure of what they're saying; indifference, where they act bored, shrug, or have no facial expression, hiding the emotions they feel; and overthinking, where they seem like they're working on a difficult calculus equation in their heads, instead of telling a story that should be easy to recount *if it were true.*

Have them tell you their story in reverse. This is a more active and better way to uncover their lies. There is research that has shown when you ask people to walk you back through their story, instead of in chronological order, it's easier to tell when they're lying. This is because the brain now has double the work, and is so focused on getting it right that it can't be bothered with trying to cover up verbal and nonverbal cues that suggest deception. It's a lot more difficult to lie than it is to tell the truth, and making the brain work harder will make the behavioral cues for lying more obvious.

Liars have to spend a lot of mental energy formulating the lie, making it difficult to keep track their behavior AND the way you respond to them as they lie to you. This takes a lot out of them, and so when you add in something taxing to the mix, they will crack.

Trust your gut. Sometimes, your gut reaction is the best thing to go on. There was a study where 72 participants were shown clips of interviews with crime suspects, who were just actors. Some of the said suspects were guilty of stealing $100 from a bookshelf. Yet, every suspect was instructed to tell the interviewer they hadn't stolen the money. The participants only identified the liars 43 percent of the time, and the honest people 48 percent of the time.

The researchers assessed the unconscious and automatic responses to the suspect by making use of their inherent behavioral reaction time. They found that often, the participants would unconsciously connect the words "deceitful" and "dishonest" with suspects who were guilty, while associating the words "honest" and "valid" with the suspects who told the truth. This means we have an intuitive notion of whether we're being lied to.

The question then becomes, why aren't we good at knowing when someone feeds us lies? Our conscious responses mess with our instinctual associations. So, rather than depend on the gut, people would rather focus on the behaviors stereotypically and sometimes erroneously associated with lying.

No Universal Sign for Lies

To catch a liar, first understand that these behaviors researched are nothing more than cues that *might* mean deceit is in play. Rather than looking at the usual lying signs, notice the subtler behaviors that might indicate dishonesty. If you need to, you can make it even harder for them to lie by adding pressure, asking the speaker to tell you the story again, but backward. Above all, and this bears repeating, trust your gut. It will save you needless pain and trouble. Your gut will not and can never steer you wrong if you do not let your head get in the way.

Chapter Ten: Spotting Flirters and Seducers

Flirting is such an amazing thing, especially when you're the object of attention, and the other person is just as into you as you are into them. The trouble is figuring out if they're just nice, or if really something go on that you could both explore. Maybe you're the one person who can never tell when someone is hitting on them or flirting with them. Or, you might have a problem distinguishing when someone is nice from when they're flirty. Either way, it's okay. After this chapter, you'll never have to wonder again.

Let's Play "Spot the Flirt"

Sign #1: They're different around you. Some people are overt flirters. They're into you, and you'll know it — or at least, everyone else who isn't clueless will know. Other people simply change the way they act around you and hope you notice. Pay attention to whether they laugh louder, get the quiet, joke, and talk a lot more, or become a bumbling, nervous wreck.

Sign #2: They connect with your eyes and hold them. You can tell by looking at their eyes whether they're flirting with you. There are studies that show when someone holds your gaze for long periods, it either results in feelings of affection, or it means the affection is already there. If they're making eye contact with you, and they're not looking anywhere else, then it's likely that they think you're attractive.

Sign #3: They're constantly glancing at you. Some people don't hold eye contact. They glance at you. The difference between a regular glance and a flirty one is if they glance a lot and catch your eye often.

Sign #4: There's a smile that's for you alone - no one else. If someone is flirting with you, they'll look at you with different eyes than they do others. You'll find those twin pools glinting with a heartwarming softness. If they were smiling before you locked eyes, the smile grows in brightness or intensity.

Sign #5: They make a habit of teasing you. There's nothing straightforward about flirting like this, but it happens often. People who flirt this way are trying not to be too obvious about it. They will gently poke fun at you, and offer you compliments indirectly, hoping against hope you take the hint. This teasing differs from bullying or insulting, so if you feel like they're putting you down, or you're uncomfortable, then maybe it's time to walk away.

Sign #6: They fidget with their clothes. Sometimes, they might fiddle with their outfit or hair, jewelry, even hands. Whatever they can get within reach. It often means they're nervous because you, their crush, are with them. They can barely contain themselves around you.

Sign #7: They try to discover if you're single in the sneakiest way they can. You may have heard them say something like, "Wow, does your girlfriend have any idea how lucky she is?" Or they'll say, "How in the world are you still single?" They're trying to find out if they stand a chance with you, or you've already taken, but they don't want to be upfront about it.

Sign #8: They always try to get a laugh out of you. They want you to relax and be at ease with them, so they'll joke, do silly things, anything to get you giggling and wondering if a life with them one would be full of laughter.

Sign #9: They think you're hilarious in a good way. You'll find that they laugh at every joke you make even when it's not that great. They want you to know that they like you, and they appreciate you.

Sign #10: They maintain open body language with you. They'll want to be closer to you, and to facilitate that, they will keep their body language open to you. They want you to know, on an unconscious level, that they are at ease in your presence. If you notice they're facing you, leaning in, and their feet and knees are pointed right at you, then they're probably flirting.

Sign #11: They'll react first to your posts on social media. If they keep liking and commenting on your stuff, it could only mean they want to get your attention, especially when they like EVERYTHING.

Sign #12: You notice they check you out. You know you can scope someone out surreptitiously; if you catch them doing that to you, then it's pretty obvious that they're attracted to you and trying to flirt.

Sign #13: They touch you in subtle ways. Those accidental touches aren't so accidental. They might give you a quick pat on the shoulder, graze your arm, or attempt to brush your feet or hands if you're seated at the bar or at a table. These parts of the body are sensitive and will often cause you to instinctively consider whether you're attracted to them or not.

Sign #14: They do their best to get in your line of sight. When you're in the same space together, notice if they somehow always wind up in your line of sight, or if they somehow are always close to you, but not quite. They probably want to get to know you but aren't brave enough to start a conversation or want you to make the first move.

Sign #15: They fidget suggestively. Here, if they're playing with their wine glass, or its stem, or whatever, but moving their hands in almost hypnotic, deliberate strokes as they focus on you, chances are they're interested and trying to flirt with you.

Sign #16: They keep pointing out their flaws; an odd way to flirt but flirting all the same. If they're very self-deprecating as they make jokes, then they're trying to bond. It's also the case when they do that while casting light on your own strengths. They want you to get closer and help them with whatever flaw they perceive.

Sign #17: It's all in the wrists. Do they have their right wrist in their left hand? Then they're probably sensually available. If it's their left wrist in their right hand, they're probably hostile. Be mindful of this one though, since it could be different depending on whether they're left or right-handed, or ambidextrous.

Three Steps to Successful Flirting

Understanding the way flirting works from personal experience will help you spot when someone else is trying to flirt with you. Things will probably happen in a certain way or order. Think of it as a script you follow. Say you're at the movies. You know that things go a certain way. First, you head over to the counter to get your ticket. Then you go get some popcorn and whatever else you want to snack on. Then you head to the cinema. The lights dim. The announcement asking you to turn off your cellphones comes on, and then the trailers start before you finally get to see the movie you paid for. This order of events helps to guide the way we behave and will also affect our expectations.

We also use scripts in our relationships, expecting certain behaviors to happen in a certain order. It's all usually subtle and nonverbal. For instance, you wouldn't beat your chest like a caveman and say, "Me. You. Sex. Now." Well, maybe you've roleplayed that, but that's not the point. It's probably more like you've both had a bath, one of you leans against the wall staring at the other a certain way, someone dims the lights, and then it's sexy time.

These patterns happen at the start of relationships too. Researchers Susan Fox and Timothy Perper have discovered there are three steps we all have to negotiate so our flirting can work out.

1. The approach. One person reaches out to the other. The other must respond positively, so the flirting can go on. If they don't, that's the end of that. Fun fact: Men don't like being approached from the front, and women don't like being approached from the side. For you to move from the approach to the next step, it's important that you smile genuinely and sincerely. How do you smile genuinely? Simple: *mean it.* Also, fake smiles are usually asymmetrical, delayed, and last longer than normal. Also, there are no crow's feet at the corners of the eyes. As you approach, you say hello, and you flash your eyebrow at the other person. The eyebrow flash is often an unconscious thing we all do when we're meeting someone we'd like to engage socially.

2. The swivel and synchronize. Say your approach was warmly received, then you'd need a conversation starter or an opening line to encourage back and forth banter. The last thing you want to say is bizarre, rude lines like, "Your place or mine?" "Is that your real hair?" "You remind me of someone I once loved." This stage is called swivel and synchronize because, after the approach, both parties turn so they can be face to face, and they match body movements, which means there's rapport going on. This is often a natural occurrence. Some people can mirror well, but look from their waist down at their lower legs and feet to figure out if they're interested in you. Remember, their knees and feet will be pointed your way if they want this to go on. This step also lets you look into their eyes, so you can tell by the dilation of their pupils if they're interested or not.

3. The touch. In this phase, one of you touches the other, and the other has to welcome the touch for the conversation to continue. Touch matters a lot for building rapport. At this stage, there's listening, talking, mutual sharing, and humor involved. According to Fox and Perper, women touch first, more often than not. That mutual sharing is also important, because the more people share with you, the more you like them, and the more they let you share with them, the more you like them. This is all backed by research. When at this stage, there's going to be humor. In opposite-sex flirtation, research has shown that interest in dating is more about the laughter that the woman gives, more so than the man.

Again, this is not some pick-up artist guide, so please don't run around trying to force these things to happen. The whole pick-up scene can be sleazy; avoid it if you're all about genuine connections.

You should have no problems figuring out who's flirting with you and who isn't now. Flirting can be fun, given the right conditions and with the right people, so, enjoy yourself responsibly.

Chapter Eleven: Identifying Mass Manipulation and Propaganda

We have the late, great intellectual Noam Chomsky to thank for first pointing out the strategies that the media uses to manipulate us. Ever since he wrote about them some three decades ago, the media has only developed even more ways to get to us. We now have Facebook, Instagram, Twitter, and so many other sources of information they can use to get us thinking in ways that benefit the viewpoint they hold. Sadly, the influence they wield isn't always for good.

Media Manipulation Tactics

Tactic #1: Create a diversion. This is the media's go-to ploy for manipulating its audience. They take important information you and I need to know and wedge it between a lot of inconsequential stories. It's even easier for them to do this now that we have the internet. (At least we have the option of simply filtering out parts that don't matter to us.)

Tactic #2: Blow a problem out of proportion. When they make a huge enough deal about something that probably isn't a huge deal (if we'd all stop to think about it), the media can get a rise out of society, fostering huge consequences. For instance, NASA put out an article in 2016, claiming that if there were any science at all to astrology, then the zodiac signs would have to keep changing their positions. A Libra would, at some point, be a Leo, a Scorpio, and so on. So, what did the popular Cosmopolitan magazine do? They put this claim out there like it was an actual scientific discovery, saying that 80 percent of people must switch zodiac signs. This went viral, forcing NASA to print a retraction.

Tactic #3: Poco a poco. In English: Bit-by-bit. When the media wants you to view things a certain way, it publishes its news materials bit by bit. For instance, if they wanted you to believe that the earth is flat, they wouldn't create a headline: Breaking News! Earth is Flat!" Not unless they don't feel like being in business any longer. Instead, they would start you off with a story about how some NASA satellite found a few flat planets just outside of our solar system. Then they would tell you that another version of Earth has been discovered in orbit, that it is flat, and has people on it. Finally, they'd wrap up with, "Hey, so, all the equipment we've been using to view the Earth from outer space all this time is super faulty and outdated. These newer telescopes now show that the Earth is flat." Yes, this is a ridiculous example, but believe it or not, the media has *that much* influence, and this strategy works. The media also uses this bit-by-bit strategy to create new habits or a "new normal" (sound familiar?). This is how they normalized smoking in the 20th century.

Tactic #4: Postponing. If the media wants you to have to make a tough decision, they will present it to you as "painful, but we don't have a choice." Next, they will let the audience know that they have to make a decision tomorrow, not this red-hot minute. It's easier to deal with sacrifices when you know they're coming, versus when they're staring you in the face.

Tactic #5: Kill them with kindness. You will find that advertisements geared toward children have a certain vibe about them. They use symbols, language, intonations, and arguments, all carefully crafted to make sure there is no criticism. You will also notice that brand slogans and ad copy use the imperative form, meaning they sound commanding like you don't have a choice. They also target you in the emotions by triggering basic feelings like fear, greed, the need to be a part of something, the need to feel a cut above others, and so on. This way, you find yourself making impulsive decisions, and you can't for the life of you figure out why.

Tactic #6: Emotions means thoughts off. A friend told me that in journalism class, they were literally taught, "Bad news is good news." That's the media. They are all about working up your emotions negatively so that you are blinded from the facts. You can't think objectively because they've done such a neat job of blocking out the rational part of you. Now, you see the version of reality they want you to see. This is the reason smear campaigns work. The next time you see someone being actively maligned by the media, hop on YouTube, and look for the speech taken out of context — preferably from a YouTube channel that is not mainstream media. You'd be surprised at what you notice. Information warfare is still a thing. Learn how to not get involved by turning off the TV, then asking yourself what emotions you feel, why you feel them, and about the facts.

Tactic #7: Un-inform sheeple. The media, along with the government, can actively manipulate the populace because most people do not get the mechanics of these manipulative techniques. Often, this is because of a lack of awareness. They are uneducated about the fact that no, the media is not your friend. It's serving an agenda, and that agenda probably doesn't serve you. According to Chomsky, the information that gets to the elite is a lot different from the information the "hoi polloi" gets. Thankfully, things have changed since his time, and now we can readily access alternate sources of information so we can judge the facts for ourselves. You don't have an excuse anymore to fall for the media's shenanigans.

Tactic #8: Feed them crap and make them love it. The media encourages people to stop thinking and to be more accepting of things that ordinarily, we would immediately dismiss as harmful or worthless.

This is why we are inundated with so many movies, shows, sitcoms, tabloids, and all sorts of entertainment. It's not just for the harmless purpose of recreation, contrary to what you might assume. Entertainment is a great way to make sure that we're not looking at the problems looming over our shoulders, and by the time we do, it will be too late.

Tactic #9: The guilt trip. The strategy is simple. Make people assume they're the ones to blame for everything going wrong in the world. Let them blame themselves for things people did centuries ago. Make them blame themselves for the wars that governments spearheaded without their permission or support. There was a photo of a boy lying between his parents' graves that went viral in 2014. It was depicted as a picture from a war zone. In reality, the boy had taken the photo for a project showing love for his relatives. *Media at its finest.*

Tactic #10: Know them better than they know themselves. The media makes a point of learning all it can take about everyone, and in the process, they go overboard. Back in 2005, a British tabloid named News of the World was caught doing something so brazen and dastardly that it boggles the mind how they even thought they could get away with it for long. They were wiretapping politicians, celebrities, and members of the royal family. This was how they wrote so many "exclusive" articles, which pulled in a lot of readers. The tabloid was buried in lawsuits from ordinary people and celebrities, and after paying whopping amounts of compensation, they shut down.

Social Media Manipulates You Too

You might make a habit of checking all your feeds, but then, it would probably surprise you to learn that really, most posts do not accurately depict actual views held by actual humans. You know your cousin Betty is as real as they come and not some AI somewhere, but social media can un-inform you, misinform you, and mislead you. There is a lot of evidence that social media platforms make use of your data for other purposes, and this has been the practice even way before they officially came out with Facebook ads and Twitter ads. Bots and trolls are on these platforms, used solely to manipulate the way you think.

Tips for Dealing with Social Media

1. Do not trust them. You might be doing yourself a huge favor if you only followed the things that serve you and friends you do know. Facebook data was used in manipulating voters in the 2016 election; a scary thought. You would be better off not trusting these companies with your data unless they prove that you can. Be mindful of the content you like, or don't even bother with the "like" button. Whatever works for you. The less they know about you, the harder it will be for them to manipulate you.

2. Know your own perceptions. You don't want to be a part of the manipulative machine that is social media. There are a lot of biases we all have with our thinking, and these big tech companies know well how to exploit them. So, what should you do? Find all possible viewpoints on a subject. When you google something, don't just look at page one. Go all the way to page ten (or farther, if you can.) Better yet, after googling, run that search phrase through DuckDuckGo. You'll find that there's some interesting stuff you don't see on Google. Be quick to question any story you see out there, rather than "like and share" automatically.

3. Beware the power of bots. They are great at shifting public opinion to whatever the creator would prefer. MIT professor Tauhid Zaman demonstrated how Twitter activity surrounding politics would be a lot different if there were no bots on the platform. It's not about the number of bots. Their strength doesn't lie in numbers, but the number of posts they make.

4. Make a point of engaging with actual humans. In-person. You will feel a lot better about it. "Social" media isn't so social. It takes away from the benefits of having a real, live human to talk to. You feel even

better when you connect with people right in front of you, not people looking at a screen like you are.

How Deep the Rabbit Hole Goes

Governments are actively making use of social media to manipulate the public. This begs the question, is democracy still a thing? Propaganda is nothing new. However, what makes social media worse is that it makes it easier to spread toxic messages on a worldwide scale. It doesn't help that now there are advanced methods to target specific users and to make the message even harder to get away from.

The University of Oxford's Computational Propaganda Research Projects says that shaping public opinion with automation, algorithms, and big data (computational propaganda) is now a part of our day-to-day life.

In its third yearly report, the project considered what it dubbed "cyber troop" activity, spanning 70 countries. In case you're wondering, cyber troops are what they sound like. It's the term used to describe actors representing the government or political parties, who manipulate public opinion, spread messages that are divisive, attack any political opponent, and harass all dissidents as well.

2017 saw a 150 percent surge in the number of countries with cyber troops launching these computational propaganda campaigns. The reason for this growth is that the masses have become a lot more sophisticated. They're better at being able to spot trolls and obvious manipulation. Another reason this is growing is there are countries only just getting the hang of social media, just now playing around with these computational propaganda tools.

Researchers found there were 56 countries with cyber troop campaigns on Facebook, which makes Facebook the king of the digital propaganda pile. Facebook works well because they've got the most users, and they can connect to not just you but your family, friend, and maybe in 2025, your neighbor's dog.

There is also cyber troop action on YouTube and Instagram, and WhatsApp. It is assumed that in the coming years, political communications will increase exponentially on these platforms. It doesn't help that it's not quite as easy to supervise video content as it is to supervise text, so the chances these fake videos can be taken down aren't looking too good.

When you're on social media, you have to know three kinds of fake accounts:

    • Bots, which are very automated and designed to imitate human behavior on the internet. Often, these are used to drown out anyone who disagrees with a viewpoint or to amplify a narrative.

    • Humans, who create more fake accounts than bots, and post tweets, comments, and also "slide into your DMs."

    • Cyborgs, which are a blend of humans and bots.

There's one more fake account type: The stolen or hacked one. If an account has a high profile and a lot of followers, then they're extremely attractive to people looking to hijack them for their own purposes. They use these accounts to spread messages supporting the government's propaganda. Other times, these accounts are simply hacked to keep the owner from expressing their viewpoint.

Here are some scary stats: 87 percent of countries make use of accounts controlled by humans. 80 percent of them use bots. 11 percent of them make use of cyborgs. 7 percent of them use stolen or hacked accounts. 71 percent of all these accounts often spread propaganda that's pro-party or pro-government. 89 percent are set up to start smear campaigns or attack all opposition. 34 percent spread divisive messages to break people up into factions. 75 percent use media manipulation and disinformation to deceive users. 68 percent use trolls sponsored by the state to take shots at journalists, the opposition, or political dissidents. 73 percent flood social media with hashtags to amplify whatever messages they want.

22 Propaganda Techniques You Should Know

1. Stereotyping or name-calling: The idea or victim is given a terrible label, that is easy to remember and sounds pejorative. This way, the audience automatically rejects them without giving much thought to what the label represents. Examples of such labels: "Tree-hugger," "Nazi," "Special Interest Group," "Snowflake."

2. Glittering generality or virtue words: These are words chosen to trick the audience into accepting people or ideas without thinking much about the facts before them. Examples: "Organic," "Sustainable," "Scientific," "Natural," "Ecological."

3. Deification: This is making an idea or person into a god of sorts. They paint them as sacred, holy, or special and above all laws and conventions. When the opposite of this person or idea is presented, they are painted as blasphemous. Examples: "God-given right to..." "Gaia," "Mother Earth."

4. Transfer (Virtue or guilt by Association): A respected symbol that has authority, prestige, and is sanctioned is also used right along with a different argument or idea so it appears to be just as acceptable. Examples: University Seal, American Flag, Medical Association Symbol (or something akin to it).

5. Testimonial: A respected personality, or someone who is loathed, comes up to say that a product or an idea is good or bad. This way, the public doesn't look at the facts, but only focuses on the character of the person describing the idea or product.

6. Plain folks: This is a method of convincing the audience that an ideal is actually good because this same ideal is upheld by "other people just like you." They will use phrases like, "Most Americans...," "This is the will of the people," and so on.

7. Bandwagon: This is when the media wants you to accept what they're saying, by letting you know if you don't, you'll be missing out on some great benefits. This is used a lot in advertising. You'll hear

phrases like, "Be the first among your friends," "Act NOW!" "Miss it, miss, out!" "This is the next big thing." Ask yourself if anyone else among your friends actually want sot to buy into the garbage you're being sold to snap out of that trance.

8. Artificial dichotomy: The media will try to get you to accept there are only two sides to a problem, and each side needs to be accurately represented for us all to make an honest evaluation. This dupes you into thinking there can be one only right way of looking at things. This works by simplifying reality, and then distorting it, to the media's advantage. Consider the controversy of "evolution" versus "intelligent design."

9. A hot potato: this is a question or a statement that is untrue and designed to elicit anger so that the opponent can be surprised and embarrassed. AN interviewer may leave discussion and veer off on a tangent to ask, "Do you still have issues with your husband?" or "When will you finally pay up all the taxes you're owing?" It doesn't matter that the questions are based on false premises. It does what it should do, which is to injure the reputation of the person being interviewed.

10. Ignoring the question or stalling: This gives the chance to escape a pointed question, or to get more time. Examples of phrases you'll hear are, "A fact-finding committee is investigating this matter..." "More research is required..." "I'm summoning a body to investigate this attack."

11. Least-of-evils: This is how they justify something that is unpopular and unpleasant. "War is terrible, but it is the price to pay for peace."

12. Scapegoat: This is used along with guilt-by-association to keep the public from scrutinizing the problem. It's about shifting the blame from one person or group to another, without really diving too deep into the gray areas of the problem. You'll hear statements like, "President Obama got us into this mess," or "Trump caused the drop in employment rates."

13. Cause and effect mismatch: This confuses the audience about the actual cause and effect in play. Most things are caused by more

than one thing, and so it would be misleading to say, "Cancer is caused by bacteria," or "Cancer is caused by homosexuals in the United States."

14. Out of context or Distortion of data or Cherry picking or Card stacking: To convince the audience, the media will use selected information and not give the full story. They could put out a study that says diet sodas have been found to help with weight loss, but then you find they only studied people with an already active lifestyle, and the study was funded by Big Soda.

15. False cause or weak inference: This is when the media makes judgment but does not have enough evidence to pass that judgment. Also, the conclusion does not always tally with the evidence they do provide.

16. Faulty analogy: This is an overexaggerated comparison, like a slippery slope, where it is assumed that a slight movement one way will lead to a movement to the most extreme point that way. (Example: "Smoking marijuana leads to cocaine addiction!") They could say, "Bitcoin is surging the same way it did right before the great crash; therefore, we will see the bubble burst really soon!"

17. Misuse of statistics: They report average numbers, not the actual amount. They could say, "9 out of 10 doctors recommend...) without telling you that they literally only got that info from three out of four doctors they spoke to. They could also pull the trick of mixing proportional and absolute quantities, like this: "7,600 more rats died from drinking the agave nectar tea, while with others who stuck with chamomile, had a death rate of less than one percent." They also use distorted graphs, where they might represent 7 out of 10 as 71.354 percent.

18. Fear: The media loves this one. Just tell the people that there's a threat and denounce all those not taking it seriously enough, as you accuse them of being unpatriotic and putting everyone else in danger. People will get scared, and they will fall in line.

19. Ad hominem attack (Deflection): Rather than attack the message, they attack the messenger.

20. Tu quoque attack: The media responds to their opponents by saying they are using a propaganda technique, or a logical fallacy, rather than focusing on their opponent's evidence and argument. They basically accuse the opponent of doing what they (the media) are actually doing.

21. Preemptive framing: They frame the issues the way they want people to perceive them. An example of framing would be, "The only reason we're having trouble with the economy is that the Dems were too busy doing anything but fixing it." Again, no effect has just one simple cause.

22. Diversion: Whenever something is threatening or embarrassing, the media comes up with a diversion. You may have noticed this during the Hong Kong riots, the media was eerily silent on the matter for a long time.

Chapter Twelve: Training Your Analytical Mind Daily

Let's talk about your analytical thinking skills. How are they? For some people, these skills come naturally. For others, they must work at them. You need to be driven and interested, displaying a lot of perseverance if you're going to acquire this skill. You're going to have to apply what you learn. That's what this chapter will help you with.

Why Analytical Thinking Skills Matter

They are critical in work and in your personal life. When you know how to think analytically, you can solve problems and spot solutions that people do not consider, even though they're as plain as the nose on your face.

With analytical thinking, you're able to see when emotions are causing everyone to go blind to the actual issues on the ground. You can also tell when you're not in the best position emotionally or mentally to decide. You do not allow yourself to be pressured into acting but think things through thoroughly. Often, this saves you money, time, and energy as you know the things essential for yourself and those around you at any given point in time.

When you must gather data, solve problems, or make sound decisions, you need to think analytically. When drawing conclusions from the data you've collected, you need to be analytical and efficient in thought. This skill is very desirable when managers seek who to hire, as it instantly makes you a good fit for the organization. To excel in life, give yourself the gift of sharpened analytical thinking skills. Here's how you can do that.

Seven Steps to Better Analytical Thinking

1. Observe everything. When you go for a walk, observe your environment and the people around you. When you're at work with colleagues, observe them. As you do, make sure to use all your senses, so that you have a truly immersive experience. What is it about what's going on that holds your attention now? Focus on those things. Make sure you keep your mind engaged.

2. Read more books. If you want to do well at thinking analytically, it is inevitable that you need to read more. This is how your mind stays sharp since you always keep it running and introduce it to new ideas. Don't just read willy-nilly; be proactive about creating a strategy for reading. Also, as you read, digest what you're reading. Ask yourself questions about it. Does it make sense? Read aloud if it helps you remain engaged with what you're reading. Go nuts with a highlighter. Try to predict where the book is headed.

3. Make a point of learning how things work. Don't just go looking for solutions to why your PC volume is way too loud after that last update. Dig deeper. Find out how things work, and you will be able to comprehend the process, which in turn will stimulate that analytical thinking muscle.

4. Make a habit of asking questions. When you get curious, you get smarter. Curiosity pushes you to make use of your cognitive functions, such as memory and attention. So ask some more questions, because this is how you get better retention, memory, and problem-solving

skills. Do not ever let anyone make you feel stupid for asking questions. It's a good and healthy thing to want to learn.

5. Play as many brain games as you can. To sharpen your analytical thinking skills, you should play games that work your brain. Try Sudoku, chess, crosswords, and puzzles. Download brain game apps that will keep you sharp. You can use the spare time you have in traffic or wherever to pay them and get better at thinking analytically. The great thing is that these games are fun, and so you should have no problem being motivated to play them.

6. Put your problem-solving skills to the test. Every problem has a solution. This should be your motto. So, always welcome the chance to solve a problem. Make a fun game of figuring out several different ways to fix one problem, and soon you'll find that you're the go-to person for solving issues. Where it's possible, don't just come up with the solutions, but test them as well. See which of them works the best, and then constantly ask yourself, "How could it be better?" You'd be surprised to find that there is really no end to improvement if you put your mind to it.

7. Consider your decisions carefully. In life, we have to make decisions, whether it's quitting our job to get started on the thing we want to do the most, or it's figuring out if this is the person you want to spend the rest of your life with. You should make a point of thinking long and hard about your decisions, making sure that they are, in fact, rational. Think through the pluses and the minuses, the pros, and the cons. Where you can get it, seek expert opinions on the matter. Don't be afraid of doing research, by which I mean extensive research, not just a Google search where you content yourself with page-one answers. Also, ask yourself if the solution you've come up with is the absolute best one. Don't be afraid to listen to your inner critic, because it just could lead you to an even better solution than you already have. It's okay to take a little more time to rethink your stances on issues before you finally decide.

When it comes down to it, analytical thinking is a skill, and like all skills, the only way you do better at them is to practice and apply what you learn each day. You want to make sure that you mine the gold from every experience that you encounter.

Keep practicing. At first, it will feel like the most unnatural thing in the world. You might be tempted to beat yourself up because you feel you're no good at this. Don't give in to that feeling. Think of it like going to the gym. You're not going to bench press 34 reps of 320 pounds in a day just because you walked in, especially not if you haven't been training your muscles. In due time, you will get better.

When you do, you will find that you can read people easily, without really putting much effort into it. Your mind and your gut will align, each sense sharpening the other so that you have a better read on people. Your relationships will improve, you'll do better at work, and never again will you find yourself stuck with another person's toxic behavior without knowing how to handle yourself every moment.

Here's another book by Heath Metzger
that you might be interested in

Made in the USA
Middletown, DE
24 December 2020